The World As Is

Also by Joseph Hutchison

Poetry

The Satire Lounge
Marked Men
The Earth-Boat
Thread of the Real
Sentences
Greatest Hits: 1970-2000
The Rain at Midnight
The Heart Inside the Heart
Bed of Coals
House of Mirrors
Sweet Nothing Noise
The Undersides of Leaves
Thirst
Shadow-Light
Weathers, Vistas, Houses, Dust

Translation

Ephemeral (from the Spanish of Miguel Lupián)

Editor

Malala: Poems for Malala Yousafzai (with Andrea Watson)
A Song for Occupations: Poems About the American Way of Work (with
    Gary Schroeder)

The World As Is

New & Selected Poems
1972-2015

Joseph Hutchison

The New York Quarterly Foundation, Inc.
New York, New York

NYQ Books™ is an imprint of The New York Quarterly Foundation, Inc.

The New York Quarterly Foundation, Inc.
P. O. Box 2015
Old Chelsea Station
New York, NY 10113

www.nyq.org

First Edition

Set in New Baskerville

Layout by Raymond P. Hammond

Cover Art: "Earth Soul" (©2016, 18 x 24, acrylic on paper)
          by Raina Gentry | www.raintree-studios.com

Author Photo by Kimberly Anderson (Evergreen, Colorado)

Library of Congress Control Number: 2016933873

ISBN: 978-1-63045-028-1

The World As Is

Contents

1972–1985: Uncollected Poems, Poems from *Thirst* and *The Undersides of Leaves*

from *Thirst*

from *The Undersides of Leaves*

1986–1995: Uncollected Poems, Poems from *House of Mirrors* and *Bed of Coals*

from *House of Mirrors*

from *Bed of Coals*

1996–2003: Poems from *The Heart Inside the Heart, The Rain at Midnight,* and *Sentences*

from *The Heart Inside the Heart*

from *Sentences*

2004–2013: Poems from *Thread of the Real, The Earth-Boat,* **and** *The Satire Lounge*

from *Thread of the Real*

from *The Earth-Boat*

from *The Satire Lounge*

This book is for Melody,
Susannah, Shannon, Brian, Pepper, and Bodhi

2004–2015

New and Uncollected Poems

Crayoned Rainbow

Susi, age 3
(for Susi, 30-some years later)

Across the gray-white, blue-lined
paper sky, her crayoned rainbow
sweeps. Under it, egg-shaped
figures totter—scribbled green
with swirled orange eyes,
or blue with brown mouths
and legs like twists
of thin smoke. Fatherly,
I ponder the teachable scene
and point. *Who's that?*

That's the Daddy.

I point again. *This one?*
(Tiny at the tether end
of the Daddy's long arm—
her baby brother, maybe.)
Is this the son?

No! Frowning.
That's a girl.

And this? (Up in the clouds.
It looks like a Frisbee.)
Is it a Frisbee?

She half
snorts, half sighs.
That's—the girl's—hat,
then adds a few scribbles
to clarify its hatness.

A hat, I say. *In the sky,*
I say. *Did someone
throw it there?*

21

She dons
her patience face.
*That's her hat
she's* dreamin' *about.*

I admit: sometimes
wonder takes me,
and I see she's a miracle
happening in secret—
the way mist-laden air
unlocks the colors
occulted in sunlight,
lofting them out
over the Earth,
above our heads—
as her sketch explains.

I tell her, *The Daddy
looks a little sad.*

Her eyebrows knit
around a new thought.
*'Cause he don't have a hat.
But look at the flowers!*

Pretty, I say. *They're all
the colors of the rainbow.*

Now she grants
a quick smile. *That girl
growed those rainbow flowers
for her Dad.*

Household Gods

*It was once the custom to sit on long benches
by the fire,
And believe the gods were present at the meal.*
—Ovid, *Fasti, Book 6*

Saturdays then were made for sleeping late.
No alarm clock when I was seven, just a salt
smell of bacon sizzling in Dad's iron skillet,

eggs crackling in a puddle of butter, toaster
popping up slices Mom would paint with jam.
Too often I'd stay awake into the wee hours

reading Little Golden Books by flashlight
under the covers. *Rootie Kazootie, Detective.*
The Little Engine That Could. I'd chuckle

at the stumbling dance of villagers, glued
by their greed to Dummling's golden goose.
After such nights I'd sleep past breakfast,

through Tom Terrific and Looney Tunes,
dreaming of being Red Riding Hood's wolf
hauled down flailing in the river by stones

the woodcutter had sewn into my belly.
I'd gasp awake, my heart a thrashing fish,
to find the sun high up in the shifting net

of the backyard elm, and Mom's Hoover
keening in the living room, and the scrape
of Dad's shovel blade outside in the garden,

and on the Formica kitchen table, a plate
wrapped in crinkled foil to hold the warmth
of what my household gods had made for me.

First Bird at First Light

The trilling of your solo
piccolo flows like the cool
well water Dad pumped

into the zinc bucket I held
up for him, out behind
our rented log cabin

in a breezy aspen grove.
Where, I wonder, was
that grove, that cabin,

that creaky iron pump?
Each day at dawn
your song calls back

that moment of flurried
sun and shade—and I
wonder. But then,

as just now, you stop,
and however hard I listen,
the sky begins to brim

with a pitiless brightness,
and the past melts back
into a maze of trees,

taking its secrets with it.

Oddments

today's weather map
says winter rain is falling
on my father's grave

*

snow comes on in gusts:
the window fills and empties
past my reflection

*

windowed snow swarming: TV's grainy predawn hiss…when
  I was a kid

*

nightfall bus…from one ice-bound window a woman stares
  :: stopped clock face

*

cliffside veined with ice
the sun's too pale to melt
this New Year's morning

*

May's first mosquito,
play on! I like your dreamy
one-string violin.

*

high-country storm wind shakes out sheets…wet white light
  :: | :: mother-shaped thunder

*

rain-steps at midnight—
a perfume of wet earth crawls
in bed between us

*

purple-haired shop girl,
tongue-stud touched to upper lip—
trying to make change

*

old dog's seizure past,
he paces, panting—more lost
being lost at home

*

cliffside daisies swing
from a pinch of dirt: hold on,
hold on, my heart says

*

heron on stick legs,
spread wings edged by sunset—
long day, many fish

*

iron graveyard gate
broken by morning glories:
I pause…walk on in

At Willamette National Cemetery

for my father

The symmetry of this cemetery—
        even in death
                the warriors

strictly formationed, at
        supine attention. Gray
                granite plaques flat

in the drenched
        grass. At first I thought,
           You deserve

something upright—something
        marble, the faint
                rose of just-dawn

over the tarnished
        waves you sailed
                in what others called

"The Good War." You cared
        nothing for monuments, though;
           never (as I

remember) used the word *heroic*
        for anything you or
             anyone

did back then. It was just
        unjust necessity
                that earned you this

plot, this plaque, this little flag stuck
        in the sod a few days
                each year. Is that why

you chose this place? Preferring
     to have your name
          carved on flat gray

stone, anchored in a slope of neatly
     mown grass—preferring
          to any standing slab

the monumentally self-effacing
     drift of this
          rainy late-May mist.

A Bust of Janus Speaks

A version of Borges's
"Habla Un Busto de Jano"

No one who opens or closes a door
fails to honor the memory of Twoface,
who oversees all. I survey horizons
of unsettling seas and settled lands.
My two aspects perceive what's past
and what's to come. I see them both,
both rife with swords, discords, and evils
Someone could rub out and hasn't rubbed out
nor will ever rub out. Lacking both hands,
I'm transfixed in stone. I couldn't say
exactly if it's future strife I contemplate
or conflicts in some distant yesterday.
I see my ruin: the truncated column;
the faces that can never face themselves.

The Things That Carried Them

Mother.
Cradle. Bassinet. Crib.
Shoulders. Snugli. Stroller. Car seat.
Pull sled. Saucer. Double-bladed ice skates.
Tricycle. Pedal car. Shopping cart. Scooter.
Monkey bars. Teeter totter. Swing set. Slide.
Training-wheel bicycle. Roller skates. Pogo stick.
Cottonwood treehouse. Willow-branch swing.
Bumper car. Ferris wheel. Flying Eagle. Paddle boat.
Carousel. Roller coaster. Tilt-a-Whirl. Scrambler.
Rowboat. Rubber raft. Aluminum canoe.
Skateboard. Ten speed. Snowboard. Skis.
Mini bike. City bus. Daddy's car. Beater car.
Chevrolet. Volkswagen. Datsun. Subaru.
SUV. ATV. Crotch Rocket. Chopper.
Sailboat. Bass boat. Bowrider. Jet ski.
Parasail. Parachute. Hot air balloon.
Helicopter. Gulfstream. Seven-forty-seven.
Booster rocket. Space Shuttle. SpaceShipOne.
U2. F-15. B-1B. C-130.
Stretcher. Gurney. Wheelchair. Crutches.
Stretcher. Gurney. Body bag. Coffin.
Coffin. Coffin. Coffin.
Earth.

A Conflict Photo

framed so tight we can't
tell if that fat fly's poised

on a moist rose petal or
the half-closed eye

of yet another child
(the same child always)

killed in whoever's
latest just war.

Dream Bird

He finds it by a low stone wall. Black with white under-wings, a narrow head cranked back as if to pluck the busy ants from its ruined feathers. Leaning on his father's old shovel, the one with the splintery handle he thought he'd thrown away, but he found it today in a cluttered corner of the garage and now pauses awhile, then works the blade tip under the rigid creature, scoops it from the earth, and flings it up the mountainside. The bird revolves like a chunk of charred wood amid a shower of grit, and just before plunging into the long, gray-green summer grass it bursts open. A flurry of paper. Dollar bills.

He is surprised that he's not surprised....

Now one of the bills blows back toward him and at his feet snags in a clutch of mullein. He picks up the bill, recognizes the balding head in its ornate oval frame, the impassive eyes, the smile thin and bitter: his face. And below it, a serpentine scrollwork banner: *In Blood We Trust.*

Augery

The tractor roars. A few of us
flinch at the viewing holes, then
lean in again, touch our noses
to the wire mesh.
                The big tractor
roars once more; its massive auger
twists, shakes, sinks a few inches,
jams. The engine coughs up black
exhaust…and a red coal flares
in our brains: the Earth's too tough!
But no: they flood the hole with water,
and the great screw spins.
                    They'll stab
pylons deep as the glass tower needs
not to fall. The other foundations,
the ones that will crumble, are
inside us: stupas, kivas, parthenons;
Chartres longs to lay down its ancient
stones.
        The tractor groans; its auger
wounds us. And yet we linger
like baffled wraiths
at the circles of witness.

Leaving the Financial District

He's trying to catch the five-forty bus,
walking fast, head down as always,
counting the sidewalk seams as he goes
and pondering the adhesiveness of shadows.

       Up ahead a suspicion sneaks
       black-cat-like across his path.

In his chest a feral tail bristles.
His feet imitate stones.
He sways in place....

       His gaze drifts upward
across the high-rise cliff-sides. So:
life's no benign, bewildering dream;
it's a web traversed by stealthy powers.
       He feels the stare of faceted eyes,
feels the plump abdomens dragging;
venom glitters on fangs like pretty dewdrops,
or blood diamonds, or evening stars.
       And a rough whisper brushes him:
tumblers ticking in a vault's steel door, or old
robed men murmuring oaths of office
(a faint scent of cordite clings to their skin).
       The gutter beside him brims with fluid
murky as film noir blood; leaves
sweep past, their crushed faces whirl,
the current soundless as huddled
children on porches of foreclosed homes,
hugging their knees under boarded windows.

       The choked throat of his wallet throbs.

But he tucks his head, moves on,
obsessively counting the sidewalk seams:
　　　one, two, three…
while his shadow sloshes at his feet
　　　　like muddy water washing
　　　　to and fro in a gold miner's pan.

Red Light at Rush Hour

Two garnet-eyed pigeons
scoop beakfuls of oily water
from a pothole by the gutter

where accelerating tires
drum the ramp twisting up
to the freeway. Both birds

are avid, plump as pillows,
slate gray, ash gray, a green
flush at the neck. The loud

rumbling of engines, barking
of horns and blasts of exhaust,
don't faze them. The racket,

though, means we can only
imagine their coos, the fitful
ruffling of their wings. Surely,

we think, as night comes on
and traffic thins, they must
settle on a beam beneath

the shuddering bridge road,
confide and mate, sleep,
dream—while across town

we settle into our own niche
in the far-flung infrastructure
of commerce. After drinks

and dinner, manic sitcoms
and steamy dramas, late news,
late weather, we crawl in under

down-stuffed comforters,
confide and mate, then roll
apart to lie staring at ceilings

beyond which constellations
wheel. We can just imagine
their red-shifting free fall

into the frigid reaches,
feel their shuddering fires
almost close enough to touch.

The Gulf

The marine biologist sinks
a blue-gloved hand into the Gulf,
then draws it out, stunned silent
by blackness dripping from his fingers.

===

The columnist and tele-intellectual,
known back in college as Little Georgie,
owl-eyes the moderator and shakes
off the catastrophe. "Accidents happen."
Capitalism's dangerous, he means.
Big rewards demand big risks.
Market wisdom. No pain, no gain.

===

The heron sails low over the grassy marsh,
legs stockinged up to the knee-joints in crude,
nowhere to land that isn't poison, nowhere
to stand and snap up a clean fish or two.

*

At the edge of the marsh, a half dozen
former fishermen crouch to wipe oil
off the long leaves of grass, in silence;
their Company contracts ban them
from talking to the media. Their pain
has nowhere to land, but keeps on
circling above the beloved waters,
spiraling lower as the weeks go by.

*

Tony Hayward, CEO of BP (two letters
advertised to mean *Beyond Petroleum*),
speaks freely to CNN. "No one," he says,
"wants this thing over more than I do.
I'd like my life back."
                              Later, he climbs
into a limo that whispers him away
to a throbbing helicopter, thence
to an airstrip where the Company jet
stands ready to loft him back to London,
30,000 feet over the lightless Atlantic.
In his mind he's already holding a tumbler
of Ladybank single malt on the rocks.
How many eleven-thousand-dollar-a-day
paychecks can he "earn" before the Board
cuts him loose?
                              Hell—the sooner the better!
How sweet to sway under a golden parachute,
age 54, the rest of a life in front of him....

===

Robots on the sandy bottom
saw at the pipe to ready it
for a capping attempt,
but the boil of oil and methane
keeps on thundering up
in diarrheal billows.

A sickening sight, yes—
but far from where we live.

How sad for those living there!

Our thoughts and prayers—etcetera....

===

Decaying fish at the fouled tideline—
more fish than Jesus conjured up
at Bethsaida. The Gulf's abundance
wiped out so people like me can drive
twenty-plus miles each way to work,
suckle at bottles of clean spring water,
keep our leftovers chilled for days
before finally tossing them out.

The primordial dead power the pictures
that move me to write, the underwater
cameras that make me an impotent witness.
Even the ink in my pen is implicated,
my better angels beached in slick goop
like pelicans, heads cranked back,
eyes frosted over in the wind.
Even the ink in my pen….

===

Day 46.

TV ads tout BP's commitment to clean-up.

News of a stalled rebound: unemployment, 9.7 percent.

Commercials for the new *Infiniti:* air-conditioned to mimic bucolic
breezes; the dashboard's wood hand-rubbed with silver dust.

The "spill" (a PR term meaning "eruption") stains everything.

Three thousand square miles of the Gulf's surface sheened
or slathered, the Gulf winds infused with stench.

A hundred meters down: the plumes like sprawling Rorschachs,
petro-globs tumbling like fallen angels toward the Dry Tortugas,
toward the lightless Atlantic.

Ocean floor: the very ground of Being a kind of Pompeii, sooted
over by rotting animalcules, most so holy they've never acquired a
name.

===

Day 47.

You expected,
maybe,
an epiphany….

===

The Empire once made Greece its suburb.
Then the Empire made the Wild West its suburb.
Now the Empire's made the whole globe its suburb.

Poetry: enslaved to Rhetoric,
or worse, Linguistics.

Whatever you expected
clearly will not come to pass.
Only the Gulf dying as we speak.

Only blackness dripping from our pens.

===

And yet—hypocrite poet!—here you sit,
casting your bitter lines out into the Gulf.

===

Between the I who sneers and the I who grieves,
between the one who writes and the ones who read,
between the solitary heart and nullity: the Gulf.

Against our own greed we side with the Gulf.
Against our pride, our numbed spirits, against
the gag shame has stuffed in our mouths—
we speak out. To restore the Gulf we speak out,
speak to restore, if we can, our own trashed nature.

In a tense not past, present, or future—we speak.
(We speak, said the poet, in the *possible* tense.)

Though our voices may vacillate, we speak
for the "flow of unforeseeable novelty" that *is*
the Gulf. Using words estranged by politicos,
corporatists, postmodernists, we speak up
for both the Gulf within and the Gulf without—
speaking, anyway, to make the possible possible.

Glimpse

Day by day, you long for a glimpse.

Night after night with a knotted heart
and a pinch of sighs that makes grief
more savory at your solitary table.

Yes, bitter thoughts go on battering
a naked bulb in the cellar of the brain,
where the suspect picked up at random
writhes at the hands of true believers.

But a little justice, please! Some clarity,
if only for an hour, a moment or two.

Dump out your tattered sack of urges,
obsessions, shards-of-glass slights
you've hoarded like jewels, old coins
worn smooth by the acids of your anger.

Release. Empty yourself enough to let
the world fill you with other truths.

Catbird laughter of children. Lovers
breath to breath, risking nakedness,
risking submission. Or hands bathing
blistered feet. Or the high school dropout
working two jobs to pay for the pills
that keep his stricken wife alive.

Morning sun lifting from windy water.

Your door standing open to the sea.

Meltdown

Offshore from Fukushima the dolphins glow
the color of my dreams—or, to be more precise,
their background color: a green like screens
used to transport actors from some barren studio
into the heart of darkness, or to make clay effigies
of aliens loom like redwoods, or to conjure up
from papier-mâché a massive bleeding volcano.
I watch my dreams as in a darkened theater.
Eau d'Popcorn. Bored patrons bent to smartphones,
texting just out of eyeshot. Teasers for TV shows
geared to the video-game generation. I know:
I'm bitter. But didn't I once have better dreams?
Mytho-maniacal Jungian romps á là Fellini,
truer than Truth? Well, no more. It's all
reruns with numbing commercials, dumbed
down revenge tales with machine-gunned hunks
whose faces—when the ski-masks get peeled
off like condoms—are always handsomer
than mine. Somewhere, though, somewhere
there's a glowing boy astride a glowing dolphin,
two friends fleeing the meltdown over silver waves,
under sunstruck billows of cloud, with mermaids
singing each to each, at first—and then to me.

The Greatest Show on Earth

The clown car careens into the bright-lit
center ring, buzzing like a baby chainsaw.
Smoke corkscrews from the tiny tailpipe,
the horn bleats and squalls. Now it brakes,
fishtails, skids sideways and heaves to a halt,
rocking on lackadaisical springs. The motor
pops and sputters, the tinted glass doors

stay shut. The audience leans forward.
Nothing happens—only spotlight beams
sweeping over, away and back. And soon,
frustration crackles in the bleachers. Gripes,
scattered curses, threats. Nothing happens!
Inside the car's a motley gaggle of eager
Armageddonites, ex-CIA think tankers,

talk radio megastars, flaks for Big Oil—
all playing rock, paper, scissors. The victor
gets to clamber out and take first crack
at deceiving the crowd. Oh, how abashed
they'd be to find the Big Top almost empty!
Just a few gloomy diehards left, their eyes
and nostrils stung raw by exhaust, lungs

too choked for cheers. Imagine the rest
headed home: toddlers riding their parents'
shoulders, the older kids kicking leaves,
all gazing up past bare birch branches
into the red-shifting heart of inexhaustible
openness, the profusion of its forms, feeling
small and glad in the star-spangled night.

Touch

"...as though all life were death."
—Ferdowsi

I

"If all you have is a hammer, everything
looks like a nail." Say it: Implements speak.
Thus guns whisper to ruptured psyches: *Touch
me all over. Feel how I quiver with the fire
damped in us both. Hold me,* breathes the gun.
Trigger our one desire—and I will raise you up.

II

A street punk fucked my friend's son up
for his wallet and a thrill. *Pop-pop.* Everything
bled out: past, future, Furies, gods. The gun
barked, and the stars forgot how to speak,
and silence poured down on my friend like fire
as he reached out for what he could not touch.

III

Have bloody entertainments murdered touch?
Facebook bullying? Torture by proxy? Look up:
the sky that seems so empty is, in fact, on fire
with being. We imagine emptiness in everything
to break the shackles of desire, the longing to speak,
to *be.* Emptiness absolves as it thunders from the gun.

IV

Mailman, mailman, where's my gun? My gun,
my flex-tip ammo, my 30-round mags. (A touch
of manic cunning's trained him not to speak
such litanies out loud.) Who can say what's up?
Even the scheming shooter can't grasp everything
he aims to do; but he'll at last feel real when he fires.

V

As a kid I watched Davy Crockett by the campfire:
coonskin cap, possum stew, his muzzle-load long gun
propped against a Hollywood pine. How everything
glowed! How fondly the frontier king would touch
Old Betsy, slowly swab her barrel, then snatch her up
to kill some red marauder with nary a line to speak.

VI

They bleed in theaters, temples, schools; they speak
no more, love and dream no more. The same fire
kills them in cubicles, parking lots, alleys, up
in the boardroom, down in the lobby. Only the gun
doesn't bleed, exists to penetrate what it won't touch,
what the shooter won't touch—which is everything.

VII

Touch matters. Say it! Tears well up in everything.
Touch them. Stroke skin, not steel. In the mirror, touch
the Other's face—a fire that will never speak from a gun.

Still's Figure Speaks

Clyfford Still's PH-295 (1938)

I kept trying to plead with him.
No point. A spirit had his ear,
some wheedling *Zeitgeist*.
He couldn't hear my shouts,
my cries, my howls of anguish.
I came across as a memory
of wind, I think, keening
out of the plains and gullies
of his childhood. "Behind
all my paintings stands
the Figure," he once said.
Meaning me, swaddled
in blue flesh, which he then
ripped open to show the ribs,
unhinging my jaw with his
cold palette knife. Who
was I to him? What threat
did I pose that he felt driven
to drive me like a spike
through a hand, deep
into the Invisible? I think
he loved only essentials,
as Plato, my first lover,
loved Forms: *chairness*,
not the chair itself. Clyfford
wanted his convulsive shapes
and colors to contain me,
save me from touch (and so
himself). He couldn't hear,
and now he'll never. So why,
I wonder, do I keep hearing
my exiled voice call out:
"*Miserere nobis*, dear ghost,
damn you! *Dona nobis pacem*."

Revenant

Thin fire flickers in the nest of old news
and skeletal sticks in the grate's cradle,
wrestling its own torpor as it strains
to lift the damper's load of solstice cold.
Consider how it dozed in the starter's
flint, then sparked out, unfurling a blue
plume on the flowing gas. Look

how it twists, struggling not to fail
at enlightenment, now that this hearth's
provided a place to thrive. You kneel
on the bricks, bend close, and blow
breath after breath over the hiss
and twitch of the flamelet—until it
stretches, flutters, flaps up in a *whoosh*

of fresh existence. The kindling crackles.
Splits of pine feed the blaze. Now a burst
of sparks—hints of renewal that scatter,
flaring, up the flue, to climb the steep
night in your mind…though you know
they're already sifting back like black snow
onto the rocky hillside veined with ice.

Mortal Desire

Rain started falling as he sank toward sleep. He climbed down the braided sound of it, through a hole in the roof of an enormous cavern. The rain-sound ended before his feet could touch the ground, but he clung to the memory of it for a long time before giving himself over to gravity, or whatever it is that draws us toward the center of things. They say that if we don't wake from a dream of falling before we hit the ground, we'll die; but this is a day-thought, so it didn't occur to him. He fell without anxiety, turning slowly, aware that all around him in the darkness others were falling: thousands, millions…all drawn downward by the same invisible force. A flash of lightning made him momentarily transparent as he fell, and thunder grumbled in his heart. "What heart?" he cried—then woke with a jolt. The rain had stopped, and the storm had moved on: he could hear distant thunder and see, through a gap in the curtains, jags of brilliance dancing over the mountains. But these images, in fact, were merely the final ejaculations of mortal desire. His fall had ended inside the dream. His wide-open eyes saw nothing now, and his ears were deaf to the rain that would fall with intermittent fury through the whole of the night and part of the following day.

Watch

The second hand sweeps;
the minute hand merely creeps;
the hour hand seems to sleep,

but no: *the hours like slow*
tears fall; the sweet days go;
years flow away—shallow

words whose truth runs deep:
the watch shall never keep
what we want it to keep.

Grumpy Old Man

I feel for this roof rat
that all week turned up
his nose at my traps
and poisons, but finally
couldn't avoid December's
subzero cold: overnight
he crept out to meet it
in the middle of our garage.
Now—paws clenched
like goathead pods,
each eye a pinch
of want—his face
is a mask of sacrifice.
To what? Not the likes
of me, I think, as I scoop
him with a hand spade
into a paper sack
and toss it in the trash.
Non omnis moriar, my ass.

Watch Repair

You see him through the locked glass entry door: the watch repair-
man, good and drunk. His head sways above the crossed arms he's
planted on the scarred worktable, beside the fat Chianti bottle. His
half-mast eyelids flutter as if to parry the thrusts of the flickering
desk-lamp. Glints of impish implements: hobgoblin awls, gremlin
wrenches; fragments, too, of the vintage pocket watch you left to be
fixed: gears like those that must work dragonfly wings; coiled springs
clipped from King Lear's beard; a few garnet droplets of fairy blood.
You ought to feel angry, seeing your late father's Hamilton gutted,
scattered, exposed; but now the repairman's head—like a huge,
blown poppy—sinks down onto his arms, bear-paw hands gone slack
as gloves...and a sudden tenderness takes you. To think that hulk
could handle those tools! How painful must be his love of preci-
sion, how subtle his soul. Perhaps (you tell yourself) he was digging
through all those levers and pinions to locate the source of time
when the wine-god whispered his name, and now he's discovered it
but doesn't know it. And you—what do *you* know? You who no longer
have your father's watch to wind....

The Lifting Bird

It's not enough to make the lifting bird.
You have to make the whole sky, too.
And making sky requires at least a blur
of cloud, a familiar yet not hackneyed blue,
a wind perfumed by full-blown orchards,
mountains, rivers, dewy fields; and the stew
of universal mortal stinks, don't forget:
corpses, self-deception, flop sweat—

I could go on. But suddenly I've lost
my sense of sky. Can't remember back
to how stars glittered out of the past
as night came down, unfurling the zodiac
above our interpreted world. I feel dog-tired.
The bird—why bother? Without a sky…

The Bat Man

for John Todd

I once read about a man who had a cave inside him: dripstone spires, wet cathedral walls. But I never met one of his kind until I moved to the mountains.

My friend's cave is massive. Its ceiling teems with small brown bats; their peepings pepper the air. All day they chatter confidingly, nuzzling and grooming. Their eyes are black agates, their ears tuned to the keening of spirits.

At dusk they fly from the cave *en masse* to feast all night on gnats and mosquitoes scooped up along the river, on dragonflies and juicy moths. As they feed, the bats fly crazily, performing a dance at once archaic and avant-garde.

My friend's words fly crazily too, when he talks about the bats. He looks at my face when he talks, but it's them he sees. His eyes shine like those amber-lensed lanterns railway men used to swing from cabooses, or the tropes philosophers like to hang at the ends of their freighted arguments.

On our particular train, my friend and I have moved into the lounge car; we've fallen silent over flutes of amontillado. I watch him staring out into the cavernous night of the canyon, hoping to glimpse his totem in flight.

The rickety trestle, built high above the river, shudders under us, and the train's rocking unsettles me. I picture the engineer dozing up front, lulled by the clocklike tick of the wheels. He's wrapped himself in a brown velvet cloak against the cold wind off the peaks, and the glow from the instrument panel—greenish and eerily active, like the aurora borealis—bathes his hairy, fatherly face.

Sea Dream

Clang of a buoy's iron bell
swaddled by fog. Long swells
lift and lower my oarless boat.
Wood-creak. The cold's wet
slap and *slop* upon the bow:
hollow, hollow, hollow. True,
I need to wake; and yet it's this
blind drift in the mist I relish:
rocking, rocking—cradled above
an unseen current I've come to love.

The Other Life

for Melody

Considerations cross her face like clouds
shifting high up in a summer's night.
She's gathering her thoughts;
she wants to tell me something.

> It's like watching the mountain grass
> weave and unweave in the wind,
> or a hawk drift and turn above a ridge,
> aloft in its own concentration.

How is it
her beauty can always
woo me into that other life?
Metaphor: images
remembered or invented,
unaccountable music
that wells and pours
on the far side of time:
here and now.

> Once I was crossing a high plain at night,
> surrounded by mountains, and stopped for gas,
> and while the old pump's bell counted the gallons
> I studied, far southward, a bank of dark clouds
> alive with lightning—and something more:
> a full moon rising beyond.

She looks at me at last.

> And the moon, magnified, keeps
> rising, half-hidden by clouds,
> at first smoky copper,
> then bronze, then white gold.
> Now the cloudbank's edges shine;
> inside, its brilliance flashes.

She looks me in the eyes,
about to speak.
Like that.

The Outback

When I lean into pre-dawn twilight,
involved in the hush or that half-quiet
made of a clock-radio's hum, gasp
of the firing-up furnace, water's
blind gossip in the pipes (all of these
passing for silence), so that the mind
lets go of its favorite distractions—

when, that is, I've wandered off
in the outback as sunrise shimmers
up over the hills like a drawn-out
surprise—I sometimes catch my pen's
felt tip quirking among the blue rules
with a quick-witted scratchiness
like mice making nests in the walls,

and I'm taken with the notion
that something outside my control's
going on, that words are suddenly
living lives of their own, for their own
reasons, so my body's become a mere
means of assertion, and I can't help
thinking that—even with all the odd

interruptions and false starts (lapses
of power, precision, or taste)—it's so
sweet to be right here, exactly now,
engraving this groove of sounds
into the almost impossibly thin page
of an hour I'll never touch again,
except in the silence of print.

Ode to Something

Zero does not exist.

    —Victor Hugo, *Les Misérables*

Why is there something
rather than nothing?
Because nothing
never was, was ever
just a trick of math
that turned
a placeholder
into lack,
into absence—
and zero
like a ball-peen
hailstone
struck
a crack across
the smooth windshield
of speeding
reason, making
the mind's eye see
nothing
everywhere.

But nothing is nothing
like something,
something
with its amber
honeys, cabernets
and cheeses,
blood,
blindworms,
blossoms,
lips, hips, hands,
pain and rage,
heartbreak, night-sweats,
ten thousand joys

intense
and transient.
No wonder
so many dread
the sheer abundance
of something,
its "flow of
unforeseeable
novelty," endless
irruption of
forms and essences.
How can reason hope
to hang its dream
of knowing all
on such a flood?
How feed
its fantasy of mapping
every last height,
every depth, making
both beginning and end
knuckle under
to understanding?
Therefore:
nothing. Nothing
that gives something
direction, an arc
of action,
a story,
a meaning,
the way deities
used to do.

Truth is, though, we
swim in mystery
reason can't (can
never) plumb:

no beyond, only
being and somethingness:
our lives like sparks
in a vast
becoming,
bright flecks
of foam
on a breakneck river,
swirling in the world as is.

1972–1985

Uncollected Poems

Poems from
Thirst
The Underside of Leaves

Greeley, Colorado: Sunday Evening Scene

She sat straight-backed beside her brother (or
So I thought, they both
Had the same skinny lips) at
A table for eight in the green room
Of the *Gondolier* and all
Dressed up
Like she was going to a coronary.
I could tell she was nice,
Flat-chested and all, and black
Hair and horn-rimmed glasses that
Hugged her nose white.
                              She ordered
Shrimp pizza, a small
Chef's salad, side order of garlic
Bread and small
Bubble Up, and when the waitress
Left I watched her clean
Her fingernails with her fork.
                              She
Loved her family, I
Could tell by the way she angrily
Stared at her mother (another
Skinny pair of lips not to mention flat-
Chested as her son)
When the old lady made those
Savoricious sounds, gulping
Down her draw of Coors like playing some
Bacchanalian riff on
A flueglehorn.
                              Well, that girl
Had class. She ate pizza
With her pinkie stuck out like
Signaling for a turn and all the time
Dousing those fiery
Italian spices with her ice-cold
Carbonated beverage, with the other

Seven of her group talking,
Laughing and taking their time, and
Me just watching her, my own
Meal finished, check
In my hand and my waitress
Scowling at me from the bar.
                              Finally
They all got up to go and I (of
Course) followed them out. I still
Remember standing under
The green and white awning, watching
That small-town Aphrodite hop
Into the back of a blue
Pickup truck to be carried
West on highway thirty-four
With her legs dangling from the tailgate.
And in the thunderheads piled up
Like gray-black eggs over the mountains little
Trapped flashes of lightning were
Trying to dive
Head first
Into the Earth.

Fly, He Said

I am alone. Tonight
I have no friends, no lover,
The insects
Ignore me. I walk
Down a street in Denver

And there is
Only the sound of my own
Breathing as if
A silent bird were
Falling through me toward

A strong branch,
Knowing it is there, knowing it
Is
Down there, in the
Dark.

Meditation

I
The house is quiet. Only the faint
Breathing of the furnace pilot that seems
To rise from far back in the Earth.

An occasional car passes, tires
Hissing on the rain-wet street, or a dog's
Hoarse bark in some lonely corner of the night.

II
Today, again, the ornate construction
Of equations and flags for unknown quantities
And imagined nations. The hand-carved

Canoe bears a red and yellow
Ochered corpse downriver where both
Tumble and are beaten by the falls'

Watery fists, smashed and lodged
Between huge stones like bits
Of food between Stalin's immaculate teeth.

III
Today was no different, my life
Descending like a particle of dust
Through a flashlight's beam, and

Out of it, settling
Down, sinking through layers
Of air, then of earth, then of air

Again, and finally into this silent
Borderless space, my bed unmoored and
Afloat, anchorless. This house a mere

Formality. Someone new and not wholly
Unexpected has entered
My body, wearing

Sleep's striped tie and black
Bowler hat. His voice frightening
As a river loud at your feet in the dark.

IV
Tomorrow again the equations, terrible
Algebra of living, the flags, and
The poem riding low and

Heavy in the water, my body inside....

The furnace ignites, gasping
In the quiet house. My head
A weightless husk on the pillow.

Talking in Sleep

The lines are unwound the voice
glides out
and ripples start
from the bow like migrants making
for the coves of a heart
while the ship
sails on without anchor
bell lantern or rudder
with empty bottles that clink
together in the hold
like thoughts
and the captain drunk beneath the wheel

Sense and Absence

for Margaret Atwood

Her voices take shape in
the air, deepen
in color, red-orange, green

and rocks dissolve into
pure singing

dark at brain-
center the
lost hieroglyphs
blossom (Deer,

Mastodon, She-wolf and
Bear)
        "every thing

            known
            is not known" she said
            "touch me

            yes,
            I am not
            here"

Inside My Life

Midnight. The traffic's roar diminishes. Wind
takes its place. But inside the wind
there is silence
like a man gone to sleep at sixty
miles per hour. The wheel leaps in his hands
and now nothing can be done.
The iron-webbed bridge sets a huge foot down.
He wakes.
In that moment he doesn't know
what to believe. The car
can't be real, nor the scream climbing
his throat on eight electric legs.
He thinks his wife will shake him any second now.
I hear him calling her, crying
"Wake him! Wake him!"
At her touch I ram bolt-upright in bed.
I feel the room careening blindly through the dark.
And long after she has gone back to sleep,
I'm awake.
Midnight: the wind's
roar diminishes. My life takes its place.

Introgaph

On a photograph by George Krause

This photograph is a window into my own
gray weather: water ironed flat by shadows
of clouds, low hills rocky as judgment,
the gull-stained hulk of a hotel crumbling
on the shore. My voice has awakened the dust
in those rooms, slept limp as a shirt over
the backs of chairs, waiting for a body
of pure breath to fill it. Dozing, I have
heard my convictions scuttling through halls
like blank newspapers, or leaves, or lost
hands. Light haunts that air like a trance,
a vague inflection of rock or ripples. Living
there long demands power, so I merely visit.
I go to touch what I've learned to deserve,
then nail it to the wall, facing down.

Suburban Housewife Eating a Plum

She peels it with slow
surgical bites. The livid skin,
as slack as a caul, sticks
in her gullet till
three long swallows coax
it down. Then,
the wet globe balanced
prophetic on her fingertips,
she sees

only black-veined
purple meat, a fruit
like any other
plucked from piles
at the Safeway. Smaller
than a heart, it's larger
than the raw child
vacuumed
out of her yesterday
(she's still sick from that).
But her body needs
this acid, so
she kisses the round
bruise hard: it
is painfully

cold and sweet, deeper
than her aching teeth can go
—deeper than her grief—
and no doubt sour
at the seed.

The Greyhound Station: Midnight

Promises arrive,
depart, the glass doors
swing (thick
with fingerprints) open
and shut like an evangelist's
bible. A fat drunk, head

thrown back against
the dime lockers, curses
or prays at the wall. Used
racing stubs flutter
from his pocket. Outside,

the dark cocoons keep
rolling up. Drowsy, eyes
pinned like moths
by the depot's light,
the transfers worm their ways
to snack bar and toilet. My bus

and the drunk's is due:
I study his aimless speech,
the dollar ragged in his
fist. Like a rosary
or a scar
I finger my wallet,
fat with crisp green wings.

The Gift

I've a man inside me whose fingers
are translucent candles, a surgeon's
fingers, or a priest's—the nails
pared to round, pink flames.
He unties the blue threads
that lace flesh to these bones,
unwraps me like a birthday package.
Inside, the heart his touch burns
to open: containing black ash.
Of a photograph? Coil of dead hair?
A baby's tear? Mustard seed? Love letter?

Milkweed on a Windy Spring Day

From the unexplored distances of the Present
(which we call the Future) a wind
strong as this one, stirring
from its source beyond the mountains,

will rise

and our eyes will
split
wide awake:

Light

will uproot our optic nerves
and send them flying
like these syllables of silky fire

inward

over the black rain-wet earth of beginnings.

from *Thirst*

THIRST

Joseph Hutchison

Juniper Book 47

Nightworks

Each night the faces, broken up
and passed through wires,
reassemble here, in our living room.
We twist knobs to get the color right,
but the color is never right.

Soon our friends grow paler.
On the street, in daylight, they dissolve
into gray blizzards. Or at best look
past us, voices crackling
weakly from their chests as if dubbed
(we've watched their lips rush to catch up).

What is happening? And to us?
For we have embraced and kissed,
fallen still, rolled silently apart.
From the stereo, *I'd love to
turn you on*...and that hissing
in our heads like a faulty transistor.

Surely there is love enough for us all,
though it bleeds away through wires.
The Earth is soaked with squandered love!

So we build. A glass office thirty floors up
feels sovereign, its atmosphere dry,
unlike the quicksand swaddling our bones.
There, the dream that flickers
in the vacuum tubes of so many eyes
came to me:
         I raced through a jungle,
no thought but speed, no desire
but speed...flashed
like heat lightning in clouds
of circuitry, colorless, foot soles
never touching ground...

The Open Book

The window's a page of starlight
scrawled with branches; a face

mooning there, its ghost breath
blurring the script. I douse

the lamp, and the face goes out
over the city like glittering wind.

Now my body is dark in the dark,
illiterate; the unwritten book

of my soul stands open: room
in which all sleepwalkers wake.

Grace

You who are always with me
I own nothing free and clear

but I offer my voice
the color of snow

in your hands
it is water

from *The Undersides of Leaves*

THE UNDERSIDES OF LEAVES
Poems by
Joseph Hutchison

The Insomniac

The rooster's cry
bristles at the edge of
your body.

The silence puts on black gloves.

Tears roll down
your cheeks like little
glass coffins. Tonight

the assassin
will find you. He will
look you in the eyes, and still

he will wait.

Old Blind Woman

Her vision burns
backward

summer
the empty kitchen

mother's voice
calling

everyone in

and the white
bowls
the wounded cherries

in a bath of cool
pink cream

Demosthenes, Dying, Addresses His Dead Lover

I

I will tell you
of the small things that
gather
like pebbles in
my mouth. I will not

speak of them
all. The sea despises
petty orations
and my voice grows
weak.

II

Now I am
rested. Lying on the beach
I see a gust of wind
scatter gulls and
gouge nests from cliff cracks.

I am naked. I am
erect. There is no woman
here, not even
an obliging beast. And I
have always hated

my hand. Well,
there are a few clouds over
the ocean, a
last gull lifting and veering
inland and

under the abandoned
pier a batch of

dead fish float and stink. I
get up and go toward them and notice
I've gone limp.

III

I have wanted to build
a lighthouse here. A great
beacon to guide
lost ships. A straight
structure, a place
to be in during storms. But
ships no longer pass
near here, not
for years, not for years

even before
my birth.

IV

There
were words I spoke
in the silence of your eyes
I will never speak
again. Now they are
only sounds of
an ancient language nearly
lost. I
barely remember it in
my bones.

V

Maybe I've been naked
too long. My lungs
ache and wheeze and I am
forever
sucking up mouthfuls of thick
green spittle. The air
eats me alive. Women

come naked and
beat me with dead gulls when
I sleep. My

skull is full of
gnashing teeth and the sea
shouts on the pier You are going
to die! And
I have nothing

to say. At
last. What can I
say I have
nothing at all to say.

Oranges

Little Mandarins,
emperors of flavor—

sour & sweet
as all
great rulers—

& like life itself

round,
expensive,
with a bitter

after taste

Artichoke

O heart weighed down by so many wings

The Books

On the dark shelves
the books are breathing.

Moonlight slips between
their covers, running
bright hands over
the yellowed pages.

When we read them, settled
deep in private chairs,
words splash
down through our bodies
toward the Earth's
black center.

And when sleep
buries us, the deepest
stones whisper (with
the moon's voice)
to our bones.

Letter to a New Critic

Dear Ed,
       I dreamed your
beard, a blond fire, hovered
close to your hand as it
purled words across
a page, sewing up
The Scarlet Letter with
Jungian needle and thread:
embroidery of pure light. How
I envy you sometimes!

I find myself
so often squatting
in the tight round night
of my skull, knocking
noun against verb
for the sudden spark.
I fear my imagination's
not equipped with opposable
thumbs. Could it be I've
descended the Cosmic
Tree for nothing
but my own extinction?

I have made a few
poems, though—intricate
baskets and earthy vessels
well-wrought as Grecian
jugs. Someday, I'll
weave a tapestry of beings
you helped me release: hunters
along the sacred river, each
a sinuous flame
hugging
the spine's black wick...

But for now I give
you my dream (a good
omen for your book) and
this poem like a torn pocket:
everything it couldn't
hold is for you.

Yours, A for Awakening,
Joe

Something for Issa

Reading about him,
sixty-one, wife
and children

dead, their corpses turning
black in my bones, and his
last house burning

under my eyelids; now
he sleeps in the warehouse that
hovers dark behind

my body, curled
up on the earthen floor,
a bag of dry sticks:

in his dream he
hears the rusted springs
weeping in my rocking chair.

For Pablo Neruda

You held forth the pure rose

wrapping the cut
stem in the weather
of your blood
a storm
darkening
the numberless
white petals
till
heavy with color
they fell

and fall
continually

death-ripe syllables
volcanic rains
that sing
as they kiss
the black wet Earth

Belief

for James Wright

The lake is a dark
wound in the Earth: you
lean forward, kneeling,
to bathe your hand.

Poem to Be Kept Like a Candle, in Case of Emergencies

for George

We could call ourselves
friends. Things happen: we say
they have happened. Mirrors
create us, day after day,
lifting a razor,
working a toothbrush,
and every morning
the sun is
there: these simple
images amaze us. We have
pulled at the same
puckered mouths
of bottles, trembled
at the sea-shifting Earth,
felt the blood scald
while our skulls
piped like kettles; each
breaks his own walls
to sew the black
stones back
in their seams. We
have to call ourselves
friends: odd moons
in egg-shaped orbits,
pitted by idiot fists
and reflecting
what we can
of the limitless light.

Late Evening in a Foreign City

Once I believed it. *Home*
is where the heart is: a bone
prison, a knot of blue roots between
the stomach and the brain.

But there are snowy peaks
and raspberry hedges and whippoorwills
singing the sun down brilliant
in my blood. Voices
drifting like dust in this
abandoned house. Listen:
Grandmother's ancient clock is
knocking at my temples…

Alone in my skin, I am not alone.

Sunrise Off Point Grey

Clouds
low along the horizon

the way hair swept
dark gold
across her brow

in a thin green
sweater her breasts
were shadowed
faces
of listening deer

and desire
a white gull blown
out over blue waves
in my body

high
in the sun

the abandoned cries

June Morning

Sunlit room:
a breeze thumbs through
loose papers on the desk.
Shadows of poplars swim slowly on the carpet.
Small lakes on the eastern plains
drink the sky's blue
and reflections of eagles hunt in the depths.
Here, the dreaming grass
flutters in its sleep.
The steady blackbird chatter spouts
out of the flowers.
                    On days like this
some men long for a God to praise; others
doze in the nameless mountains of the body.

Invocation

The sun's milk
spills on the sky
and sparrows rocket
up for a taste.
Reaching out over

water, branches
nod in their dreams
or mine, bowed
by the downy
heads of unborn

children disguised
as peaches. Today
I sense you in
the grass mansions,
sparks of your thought

in swollen pods
of milkweed. I want
my voice to grow heavy
with nests and eggs
full of radiant

liquor. I want
to raise drunken
arms in your sleep.
To dance! Then
you might touch me—

as the lake's shine,
a trembling
embrace,
lights up these
undersides of leaves.

Uncollected Poems

Poems from
House of Mirrors
Bed of Coals

The Boutonniere

Where the spirit fails,
or the landscape runs

to desert, I plant
my two eyes. With

a dry leaf, I sever
the plump vein

in my wrist, I
let the blood fall.

The shoot comes quick
as green lightning,

a sudden bell-blossom,
throat loaded with pollen:

my voice. I pick it,
thread the stem

into your ear,
the stiff lapel of

your straitjacket. Now
you are ready (just

close your eyes)
for the wedding of

self   and   silence.

William Matthews

Written in 1987, published 1995, in memoriam

The frisk and flare of a bay mare at a gallop
sleeks up under the tongue that articulates
his lines…whose jazz peculiarizes

the plain words we've spoken so many years
that by now they are utterly saturated
with dailiness, which is no help to virtue,

no help to wholeness. But these help: each
convolved passage a fresh flowering of
bloodlines and breath. May his ten-gallon

laurels flicker long about his ears! Long
may his wit bear him onward, racing its own
riffling shadow across the desert in our hearts.

from *House of Mirrors*

Part of a Series

There was a murmur like water
draining through pipes, and he felt
he had awakened. Out the window,

a whole hillside covered
with men, women, and children
(mostly different shades
of brown) who were starving
in gray light. And that light
seemed the oddest part—

dissolving the scene
like a time-lapse film of mold
fuzzing an apple…or the way,
after late shows, Old Glory
decays into empty snow.

*

Thinned by the Sony, Enesco's
Rumanian Rhapsody woke him
truly. After a while he got up,

bathed and dressed. In the chilly
gray kitchen, he filled a bowl
from a cereal box that offered—for

fifty cents plus three proofs of purchase—
photographs of certain creatures soon
to die out. Part of a series:

"The Vanishing Breeds."

At the Arts Fundraiser

for David Guerrero

Each of their walls is adorned
with the trash of privilege. Here,
gashes of scarlet, dark blues,
and earthtones in the scalloped
force field of a gilt frame; there,
wool that's been dyed and resurrected
as kachinas, turquoise and russet,
splayed upon a warm black sky.
"We collect," the host tells us,
swerving into talk of bond markets
and interest rates.
                          I need a drink,
and quit his company, but return
later with a Southern Comfort
glowing in my fist, and examine
the walls. Glossies of our hostess
hugging Pavarotti (at bottom, a scrawl
reading: "*Ciao!* Luciano—"); another
on the slopes with Billy Kidd;
another on the golf course at Vail,
waving to us all from the arms
of ex-president Ford.
                          Suddenly
I hear the ice cracking in my glass,
and think: *They collect.* And I see
the good cause that brought me here
obliges me to face such walls, wailing
in silence like a Jew at the Kremlin,
gnawing the bone of my contention,
swallowing words like these.

Thirst

A grief springs up
at our feet
bitter black
cold water

as if from another life
where every joy fails

till our faith
in this Earth gives
way like river ice
beneath a boot

and kneeling
down in our shadow
our animal shadow
we drink

there is no end
to this drinking

Mountain Flower

for David

The way August heat makes horizons
tremble I
think of you

hummingbird whose wings
baffle and stir

there's a flower
standing by a dirt road inside me
columbine thistle or
what I can't say
for the dust of my passage whirls
around it and will
not settle

fly
through that wind you must
single out
the blossom I lost
in the narrow glance backward
of my mirror

part the petals brother
open it and drink
it is

unreal otherwise

Equinox at the Rainbow Hill Ranch

for Bill and Betty

Matted in early light, the grass
uncurls around the ankles of the cows:
damp smoke. The barn's still dark,

walls wet; the sodden beams creak
in rootless sleep; and awakened
by the wind, a fragrance of cut hay

broods over the clank of an iron bell.
Only those apple-tree limbs, bent
low, seem buoyant. I can almost hear

the round Earth whisper its stories
to the seeds, feel the season
hold its breath to listen.

Garlic

Split-lip, shrunken
pucker like a mummy's,
your savor a breath held

under the earth; biter
of tongues, sullen
flame that chars

every throat, I
taste the dry ground
you root in, taste

the eye you lift up
to the sun. You're harsh
as sea-salt baked

onto oars
that once hauled ships
to Carthage. Oh kiss

of thirsty dust,
most ancient familiar
of the dead, you've

seasoned my voice
with a smoky
residue of time.

From a Tour Boat on Crater Lake

for Reg Saner

Here, Mount Mazama crashed
into itself, its being
a storm that burned its way out.
Then centuries of rain. So that now

the pit's wider than vision admits:
the roar of our motor strikes
the far cliffs softly
as some mosquito's whisper.
Beneath us, the water's
too pure for this world, richer
than bruise or bliss. And yet
we have seen it before: how light,
returning from any abyss, is
always this color: a violet so deep

that the heart mutters
bottomless, hangs
in the ribcage suddenly heavy,
ripe with the blood's buried thunder.

Robert Emmitt

"He got hisself all to hisself."
—The last sentence of Emmitt's
The Legend of Ogden Jenks

They'd shut the blinds against the bright
April day, alive with unseasonable snow,
but the air in your room still glittered,
each second's crystal pattern unrepeatable—
a storm your face was the calm center of.
                                        Bob,
I gossiped and smiled, though your dry mouth
gaped under stroke-emptied eyes; I knew
it was reflex, yet felt somehow you'd fallen
down a well and hung there treading water,
too wise to lavish breath on speech.
Truth is, of course, you couldn't speak,
or even signal you'd like to speak.
                                Truth is,
I invented the well just now—and it stands
for my own trapped feeling, not yours.
I hated your being so shattered, so damned
reducible! And so drew a meaning image
from your stare, as if I'd read it there.
What *did* you want? Working your tongue
as if tasting the memory of gruel, or
the first time a burst vessel felled you
face down in the dirt. I remember touching
your shaved head, warm as lichened stone,
your cheeks baby-bottom smooth.
                                Truth
is, what I wished for you then was death,
easeful death. But you waited—lingered
into June, and died on my birthday. I told
the news at my party, and Joe said, "He hoped
we'd all talk about him." And we did. We do.
Old friend, both of our wishes came true.

118

Elegy for Michael, a Friend, Killed in His Car

Toward midnight I conjure the intersection:
sparkle of glass in gutters, a fanbelt
snapped, the hosed-off asphalt slick
and rainbowed with oil. Under my shirt,
a groundswell of dark breath…sorrow
and sleep banded together.
                          And his face
rises, clear as the prose mad Ireland
hurt him into, or the full moon
that followed us home from Nebraska.
The potholed roads rolled thunder
through our bones, shouldered us
toward ditches flooded with shadows….
"One summer I worked on a highway," he said.
"Listen, Joe. It was hard labor. But come
day's end, I could measure my effort:
so many yards of fresh pavement.
Not like this writing business." *Alone
am I driven, each day before daybreak,
to give my cares utterance.* I dream him
bent over his writing table, mourning
its fabulous litter. "You enter a world
and make it real," he said. I almost hear,
on his closed boat's bow, the measured
slap and kiss of the exiling sea,
bearing him toward shores of origins
and silence….
                          But my sullen heart's
own noise drowns it out. *Friends
are lent us, kin lent. All the Earth
shall stand empty.* Again, the jolt
and weave of our wandering car
on those roads, the bruised moon
low over haunted fields. I believed
he slept in the dashboard glow, slumped
against his door, but the evening's

dishevelled sparkle moved him. "Jaysus,"
said he, "it's a dark world." Now
darker still, and each breath labored,
as the clock's two spectral hands touch,
shine—then slowly let each other grow dim.

House of Mirrors

I've slept in five houses, but wakened
in one body over and over. My eyes
stung by headlights, sore-boned
at the struggling wheel, I've steered
our goods through each bad weather.
Now our blood's jazzed again
on thin air; the money's ample,
the Rockies huge. We feel
on our way somewhere.

And yet, I ache at how dreams
can swerve to a cliff-edge, wheels
holding barely.... I think
how prodigal longings are (sparks
echoed in a house of mirrors), how far
from home our destinations: Han-shan
high on Cold Mountain; Lowell
struck down in his cab.

From the Family Album

Stones on the corners of the picnic blanket, holding things down. That's their way, held down as they are by their own gravity. Not so the man and the woman who sip wine on the blanket, nibbling at bread, pâté and cheese so lightly, lightly. They look each other deep in the eyes. Now and then, they laugh without reason. If not for their bodies, they would drift off into the clear summer sky. Year after year we watch them grow lighter, until we feel afraid they'll desert us completely. For that reason, in the end, we'll hide them deep and lay stones upon them. In love's name, holding things down.

Interlude at Green Mountain Park

A few thousand yards west,
interstate; the city
a few miles east. And I've
sweated out weeks at a desk,
machine and human noise
making me sick
of listening. But here

the hills carry quietness toward evening,
the way a nurse bears a bowl of water
to bathe the fevered body. Like slanting
sunlight in which small things cast
long shadows, this silence
magnifies:

crickets spinning
dusk on their creaky spindles,
clack of locusts, the meadowlark
jazz…. And each breath
healing air to air,
pulse to music, in the deep
and hidden valleys of the chest.

The Map

for William Stafford

Again tonight your words
have come, simple as deer.
And now your moon, snowball
flung by a boy on the last clear
day of his childhood, melts

into paths under my eyelids,
filling those animal tracks
with cold light. I follow
that map, make my way deep
into the forest...until a house

built of pine shadows appears,
a blood-red door, a paned
window where an old woman
leans, dry lips pursed—my name
blooming briefly on the glass.

The Next Room

Speaking low to myself, I
hear in the next room my infant
daughter working her tongue,
wet and thoughtful. Is
she listening? Listening

to my worrying syllables,
this selfish music? Someday,
she may recall my cadence
and think it's a rush of blood—
her very own, as I imagine it

mine. But now I hear she's
sleeping at last. Working on,
I feel in my throat's well
some other's voice, as
stones in the rapids feel

thunder in their hearts—
wet and thoughtful. And if I
call it father (father
in the next room), I must
believe he hears and listens.

Internal Combustion

I'm a responsible man, and so
they load me up. Seems they think
I'm a truck with a big engine,
thick tires, strong shock absorbers:
a little gas, some water, battery acid—
they think it keeps me happy.

But it happens I'm also a lamp
with a chimney of glass
and a bellyful of golden spice-oil.
It happens my tongue is a wick,
and when the longing
flames out from my furnace heart,
I speak, and those who listen
burn. Or I don't speak:
I swallow the fire,
and it sinks down writhing
in my scrotum like some demon.

It's that demon who lights my way.
The demon they name if they mention me.
The demon who drives me around in circles,
roaring like hell, eating my own sweet dust.

Lifting My Daughter

As I leave for work she holds out her arms, and I
bend to lift her...always heavier than I remember,
because in my mind she is still that seedling bough
I used to cradle in one elbow. Her hug is honest,
fierce, forgiving. I think of Oregon's coastal pines,
wind-bent even on quiet days; they've grown in ways
the Pacific breeze has blown them all their lives.
And how will my daughter grow? Last night, I dreamed
of a mid-ocean gale, a howl among writhing waterspouts;
I don't know what it meant, or if it's still distant,
or already here. I know only how I hug my daughter,
my arms grown taut with the thought of that wind.

My Three-Year Old with His First Conch Shell

On tiptoe he reaches, hands it to me—
a polished dollop of moonlight, spiralled
as soft ice cream—and says, "Don't drop it."
His mother's voice, her caution. Or maybe
he's lived near me long enough to learn
something fearful about pretty things
that break, get broken. Oh, not by malice,
but a kind of fecklessness: how whatever
I take up can distract my grasp, any
subtle shape or mesmerizing sheen. Maybe
he sees I'm a man who lets lovely things go,
whose next lapse could silence the ocean
he has cradled in his own firm hands.

Joni Mitchell

Water falls white on the white
washed stones, fingers
light on piano or the spine
of a lover.
Sobs and exultations,
the open mouths and eyes of astounded
houses, doves
dead in mid-air, a scatter
of leaves like torn astrologies.

With her voice full of swords and blossoms,
salt and blonde honey, voice
like the ruffle of air off the tip
of a heron's wing,
she sings the scrawl of blood
and the fiery scripture
of nerves
written under the skin.

We've slept like mountains, but now
drum and saxophone swim
in our bodies,
hook-jawed salmon that leap
the black keys, dying
for the drowned genital stars,
their fine bones singing like tuning forks.

And there are guitars
overflowing like drunken goblets,
shiny sea-turtles dragging
inland, heavy with eggs. There are
sparrows dreaming in the cradles of her wrists,
and roses, and ashes, and oceans
collapsing on empty beaches, sliding
back helpless and rising again.

Saint Patrick's Day Blues

for Esther

Scratching the strings
of your guitar at the party,
shouting out blues, drunk
on my own eighty-proof
voice. Striking the sevenths,
mimicking Mike's ukelele.
Blowing it, fumbling,
losing the G. Then
finding it a fret away,
pure as the clear green marble
I found in the mud as a boy. The one
I picked up, held up in the June light.
Squinting. Eyeing the scars. Amazed
at the brightness of the scars.
I turned it in my grimy
ten-year-old hand, the marble
flickering, making a music
from the light. A music
as crazed as those
drunken blues I banged out,
scraping the strings
as my knuckles
bled…and me
not knowing it
till the song was over,
and I stared down
in wonder at my numb
and ragged fingers. Then
strummed again. The strings
gone sour with the punishment—
for which the only cure was
more: more whiskey, more
raw-handed blues. Embracing
the music. Hugging it. Holding on
tight to the scarred and shining body.

Walking Off a Night of Drinking in Early Spring

for Joe Nigg

Through the budding elm branches, eyes
of traffic lights blink red to green;
the idled traffic surges forward in the dark—

and we stagger on down the alley, joyful,
voices loud and cloudy in the cold.
Where do these hours come from? Hours

when old wounds flare, and the night
opens, and pain boils up into conversation,
as if talk can heal. The sweating bottle

drifts hand to hand, mouth to mouth—
and stars blink through branching clouds,
the blood groping darkly in our heads;

but the moon's here, too. A bright clarity
over cars and streetlamps, over houses
and leaving trees: going with us.

Wandering Music

The sky outside my window's gusty and ragged,
shape-shifting, queasy and bright. My head
crawls with blood and darkens, would peel
itself and bell-like hang, thinking *fuchsia*,

tenderly. There were fuchsias at Gold Beach
that week I read Rimbaud in a rented bed,
adrift between two foreign tongues—his French
and the argot my spirit used in poems (I believed

whatever it said had nothing to do with my life;
it didn't, therefore my anguish). I imagined
myself in Africa, or a pale version of it: secure
office work, weekends free for the *real* stuff—

that shit we writers cook up for ourselves to eat.
Yet my Africa's here, a landscape of cubicles—
doorless, fluorescent—where light-button phones
wink like idols. And my spirit has gone away

into the world: roofs and trees, then mountains,
then clouds into Utah and beyond. Last night
I was sick in the toilet, and later walked out
for a bath of sweet-cream moonlight, and thought

of the moon on the sea at Gold Beach, and the moon
in Rimbaud, the moon in my life. "You up there!"
I wanted to shout. "Yes! You know who I mean."
But I held back. And today: this wandering music.

The Trembling

Great are those hours when the trembling
stills in the hand, and the hand moves with easy
swiftness over the page, or with easy slowness
over the radiant body of a woman.

The rest of the time, it's better
not to lift a full cup of coffee
above important papers. Better not
to shave with a bright straight razor,
or stand on a ladder picking high apples.

It's better to work hard on solid ground—
digging, planting, weeding, sleeping.
Then the trembling enters the earth
like water, and the worms wiggle out
to escape the odd and uneasy vibration.

When I think how our trembling
will be squeezed out of us,
and what short work the worms
will make of our fine stillness,
I feel thankful.

Thankful for trembling, and for hours
of great calm when a ripeness comes unlike death,
and leaves us basking in the easeful radiance
of human bodies and human words.

Crossing the River

for Susannah

The sky, after last night's wind, is bright
as the eyes of a child who's learned a new song,
and she comes to her father crying, "Listen!"

So he listens. He attends. But it's hard:
to hear what she hears, he must learn to love.

I noticed a woman on the bus one day. A red
birth-shadow flared across her left cheek.
She saw me staring; we each looked down;
the aisle became an impassable river.
If we'd talked? Oh, I'd never have risked
telling her what had first crossed my mind:
"I'll bet it tastes like strawberries."

Strawberries offer their seeds
frankly, not folded away in the core.
My eight-year-old likes them with cream,
a dust of sugar. They taste so good
that she can't keep from singing,
though her cheek's plump with fruit—
which I ought to remind her isn't polite.

But I listen instead. I attend. I am
learning how to hear the beauty she hears
as she sings with her sweet mouth full.

As the Late September Dusk Comes Down

for Brian

In the grassy slush of the Fall's
first snow, my son, age three,
is dancing. He's dancing
this boot-heavy jig for joy—
or simply to drive out the ache
of an idle day indoors. He stamps
oblongs in the lumpy whiteness,
now and again gives a shout
made of steam. Then he halts
by the sagging apple tree
and stands a while, head back,
gazing through the ruined fruit,
into the failing light. Sure,
I should call him in. But I want
to savor that glad, forgiving look
that glows on his upturned face.

Cape Kidnappers, New Zealand

After a photograph by Linda Pohle

for Skip Baldwin

The child's red hat floats
just above the reeds.
The sea she walks beside reaches
toward her, curling whitely,
slipping back....

Each year a few more inches
of ash-gray volcanic soil crumble
off the cliffs, into the claws
of the waves. For a thousand years
the arbutus grove has been retreating
into the windy valley.

Far up that valley
the child's house stands—white,
slate-blue, grayish brown...door
the same ember color as her hat.
It all seems to float
just above the dark trees.

A thousand years....

When we think of it, we know
that hats and doors are
sparks brief as scarlet glimpsed
under the blackbird's wing
in flight....
One day, the sea swallows
all...and always
"too soon."

But the road home (the child's
feet know this) is long—
almost endless....
And so she walks lightly,
at ease and patient, bearing
her small flame onward
into the ancient shadows
of the hills.

City Limits

for Melody

You're like wildwood at the edge of a city.
And I'm the city: steam, sirens, a jumble
of lit and unlit windows in the night.

You're the land as it must have been
and will be—before me, after me.
It's your natural openness
I want to enfold me. But then
you'd become city; or you'd hide
away your wildness to save it.

So I stay within limits—city limits,
heart limits. Although, under everything,
I have felt unlimited Earth. Unlimited you.

Memory (II)

A clear light dreams on your gentle face,
bathes me as I watch you sleep, moves
through my mind like a balmy wind.
I remember drifting in a wooden boat
on some high-country lake: summer light
glinting off the water, and me lying back,
sun-washed, rocked by the sky's easy breath.
I must have been twelve, or even older,
allowed to row out alone and fish,
and I must have gotten sleepy or bored—
but all I remember is the calm: wind,
sun, the quiet talk of the waters.
After years of denial, years of rage,
it has found me again. The clear light
dreams on your gentle face...and I'm
drifting, drifting: watching you sleep.

Good

I might have gone on with my heart in a pouch,
as a little boy hoards his favorite marble.
I might have gotten used to dining on crumbs,
living on the faintest taste: many have done it.

I might have learned to see in the dark, if dimly.
I might have learned to disremember the dreams
of tornados, and blasted tree limbs, and floods.
I might have learned to keep smiling for no reason.

I might have denied myself your kiss, your caress.
I might have sneered, "What's happiness worth?"
I might have let my duties define my desires.
I might have hurt no one. I might have been good.

Concert at the Coliseum

Nearly two decades back, we stood
in the same cavernous hall and heard
the same music. A few months later

I would marry the woman I've left now,
and you'd go on into seventh grade.
Absurd to wish I'd have met you then—

we were different people, and life
doles out our chances at love
in its own good time. But still

I ache when I think of you there,
and me there, and the music we heard,
and the music we could not hear.

After All These Years

When I fantasize your kisses it
rattles me, like downing four
mugs of coffee in advance
of noon, making me tremble
unnervingly through the whole
lunch hour. But your real kisses,
when they come to me, calm me
like half a Valium chased
with beer, so that my convict
heart stops banging its cup
on the bars—because the iron
door has suddenly shuddered open,
and the guard's waving me out,
waving me out with a smile
after all these years.

At the Mirror

Watching you primp before getting dressed:
striped panties like sunlight through blinds,
tender curve of stomach kissing the sink's edge;
a long-toothed comb drawn through crimped locks,
then the hair dried from dark blonde to gold,
the dryer whining, blowing hard and hot;
then the eyes, the clear eyes, the lashes;
lotions, powders, sprays, to each a purpose;
and you purposeful, intent as you finish—
twist and tuck, pat and look—looking
deep into the mirror that does not love you,
as if it might reveal what only I can show you:
I who stand waiting for you to turn and see.

1995

from *Bed of Coals*

Bed of Coals

Joseph Hutchison

Vander Meer

A writer of "copy," that's Vander Meer:
direct mail letters, video scripts—
though he fancies himself an *auteur.*
                              Daily,
the early bus shakes his big dreams down
and disperses them through the tires,
into the street...delivering him up
to work, safely asleep.
                   Some clear mornings,
the routine revives his childhood fear:
learning to swim....

*

There: gulping air, though arms
sustain him...choking on
wavelets, the chlorine's cold sting
deep in the bones of his face.
                     "All right,"
snaps the lean instructor, heaving him
onto the concrete poolside. "You let me know
when you're ready to try."
                    So he sits,
gooseflesh blue, till his shameful sense
of being cast out sirens him back—
and against his better judgment
he learns how to float, how to kick,
how to hold his breath....

*

Finally, muses Vander Meer, every skill
becomes second nature...as the bus
sighs to his stop. And before he knows it
he's up,
        down the steps,
                out the doors,
on the walk...doing his tight little
breast-stroke through the crowd.

147

Con Brio

Too treble for ears, a gracenote's summons
feathered through our brains, piped us
to the pied guestbed quilt. Spreading towels
against stain, she baptized my bald homage
in water holy past pun or punishment. Our method—
pure rhythm; as a rosined bow thrills the gut
to gladden the soul, so the *lingua franca,*
pentecostal stammering of our hearts
renewed us. Spouses, friends, hurt families
only meant we'd need to stop and think—
someday. Not then. Blind joy with its wings
of breath raised us up (though I'm no Christian,
and in her the Pope's crosier had dwindled
from flute to pennywhistle)...raised us up
catholic, graceful *con brio* and fluent in tongues.

Orphic Vander Meer

As he entered her body, the first time,
she wept—but not with joy. Tremors
ringing out from her collapsing marriage
shuddered through them both. He didn't know,
but guessed the Church was crumbling too,
and the colossus she called Mother.

                                     Shaken
Vander Meer! Probing her past for the ruins
he might restore, raise up in new shapes,
new shelter. Yet how dumb he looked
in khakis, boots and pith, shouldering
a pick-ax in place of a lyre. Myopic, all
catalogs and theories, archaeologist
of love.

        No wonder she's withdrawn—
gone darkly like Eurydice—to engineer
her own new life. Was it his backward look?
Or did she bow to a deep necessity?

                                      Well,
it scarcely matters now to Vander Meer,
tossing on his bed, lost head borne
on the white wave of his pillow. Adrift
in his dream, perhaps he can remember
himself, discover a cure-all voice
to raise above the bloody lamentation
of his heart.

        Of course, we may forgive
pragmatists and Christians if they doubt it.

From an Unmailed Letter

My wife, happening upon my journal, said:
"Writers are crueler than normal people."
I argued. Yet, facing this page, I
do feel it: my willingness to wound you
with grief-sharpened praise, an impossibly
possible vision of our future in love—
when what you need, what I owe you,
is more merciful: my silence.

If I dream of awakening beside you,
why say it? Why mention some birdsong day
in June, fresh wind pouring a sweetness
of dust through the screens? Outside,
leaves twitter on twigs in the cloudlight,
their shadows bathing us…can you
feel it? Can you feel why I say it?
My will-'o-the-heart words….

I would be kinder, but speech seduces me—
itself seduced by the baths of delight
our bodies drew for us. Am I cruel,
then? Draining our lives into language
where even joy is suffering…? My love,
I suffer words for the normal joy they redeem—
and therefore hope they'll make you suffer:
you, kinder than my heart can stand.

Fighting Grief

We shared a shower, talking
and touching, the morning
after our first night together.
We kept it cool because of the heat.
I felt whole, my cough was gone,
her breasts were slippery
in my soapy hands.
The water that sprayed us
her husband owned: spray, soap,
tub and house. Only the day
was not his to keep—
our bodies, our voices,
touching and talking.
That's why, fighting grief,
I remember her wet belly pressed
against mine, her dripping
hair, the precarious
joy I felt as she gently
wiped me dry with his towel.

Pausing Outside My Apartment

Sun must be filling the room.
A bright ray is streaming
from the peephole.

Daylight and dust.

You can feel the Earth
turning under you at times.
The roundness of anguish.

Daylight and dust.

It's like a dream.
The key turns my hand.
I open my life and go in.

The Effects of Light

*"The face of the girl in the turban
was built up...almost from light itself."*
—Hans Koningsberger

I've tacked Vermeer's
Girl in a Turban to the wall
above my bed, so that she

can watch when I strip
for sleep, or for lying
back with a harrowing

novel, or a woman,
or my own sullen mind.
Gazing down now, always

about to speak, she seems
equally intimate and remote,
like the soul. I would say

she was never disappointed
in love, though whatever
became of her after posing

in this lucid window-glow is
anybody's guess. I like
to believe she lived long,

suffered well, and knew
deep joy. Yet I appeal
to her as she is,

hoping she'll teach me
my own open secret. Dear
dead girl: did he love you?

I'm tired of art, and choose
to think he loved you more
than your image, that my

happiness in your beauty
is more than just the sum
of the effects of light.

One of the Lost Moments

We sat isolated among the others.
Her feet were bare in summer sandals,
bare and lovely, that's what I whispered.
She crossed her legs...discreetly
touched a toe to my naked ankle.
We swayed like neighboring birches
whose branches wind had blown together.

When I close my eyes, I still hear leaves
weaving those wild shadows around me.

Vander Meer at Sundown

Cold wind brisk over broad lake water—
the shudder in Vander Meer's blood
as he reads: "The grave question
of how long positive values can endure
only as the aftershine of something
that has been lost."

Doing right, doing well—
morality and success—no soul
knows them! The soul distinguishes
nothing but the bright act from
the brighter...a desire
from its fulfillment.

Thinks Vander Meer, *All light's
receding from me like the galaxies.*
Too grand! The glints that needle
his stinging eyes aren't stars,
but a single star: 'Pollo Phoibee,
scattered red upon the broken waters.

Elemental Prayer in a Black Hour

1

Icy wind, lover-like mouth, drink down
this bitter cloud I took for a soul.
Sip it out through the bones of my ears
as a widow sucks tea through a sugar cube.

2

Carry off my shadow in your shadow's arms,
bleak river. Freeze me until I'm glass.
Let my failures flood and pass through me
like moonlight—leaving me empty, but clear.

3

Swallow my heart, sullen Earth, and my eyes.
I bring them to you, their dreams intact,
as neophytes once offered you seeds of barley.
Feed them your darkness. Force their sweet fruit.

4

Huddled fire, comfort my flesh—and my mind,
"which is also flesh." Let my voice rise
like smoke. Let it drift as the night goes,
seasoning the day with the scent of vanishing.

The Wound

A fresh-fallen limb, the blossoms still on—
dim stars amid the restless green. Interrupting
my therapeutic morning walk, I bent over it,
touched the tender inner wood where the branch
had fastened to its trunk.
                    Lightning?
                            Or a wind?
The limb was long, slender, smoothly tapered.
Felled by its own weight then? My fingers
crept across the moist white wound.
What a frail grain!
                    That could not bear
to bear such a profusion of flowers and leaves.

Vander Meer's Duplicity

Vander Meer at the mirror, mouth
propped wide with a gunbarrel
index finger, thinking:
"easeful death"...playing
homo ludens to the hilt. Who was it
said, a good poem always takes
the top of one's head off?

Gruesome Vander Meer! Not a little
tired of getting so weird. Peers
to find the tooth that stabs
his sleep—but as ever the ache's
general in his jaw, as if he'd chewed
his tongue's bloody rag all night.
Look, mirror-man whispers, *such
morbidity's a sign of decay:
mental*...scolding with a dogtail
wag of his finger. No no no *no,*
like Beethoven said....

Bitter Vander Meer. Half in love
with this new life alone with his art
(a cracked memoir he calls *Bed of Coals*),
half with a dream of being gathered
into artless eternity—from which sleep
what holds him back? One truth:
his heart's not in it.

This Day

On the corner, anachronistic in mid-October,
a girl in jogging shorts…tanned legs
glistening with sparse, honey-pale down,
her thighs strong, smooth as buttered rum.

How keep from staring through her to find you?

I look away, I rush past…but the wind
breathes at my ear until I taste your tongue,
dream your breasts, fingers, subtle waist—
whispers from my book of hours.
                                        All
that time scatters, memory gathers up—
keepsakes, relics, talismans. I touch one
after another like lines of print or furrows
in a face: my face, seventy…held up
by fear like a rust-flecked mirror. Did years
ravage that brow? Or the lash of your loss?
Do I wake even then with this emptiness
kneeling on my heart?
                                My own eyes
stare through me!
                        I look away.
                                        Rush past.

Yet, in flight, I blunder into it. This day:
autumn surging in the veins of each leaf,
tangled clouds above shadowy mountains,
the morning sun dazzling, remote, eternal—

how all we love will look to us, looking back.

1996–2003

Poems from

The Heart Inside the Heart

The Rain at Midnight

Sentences

from *The Heart Inside the Heart*

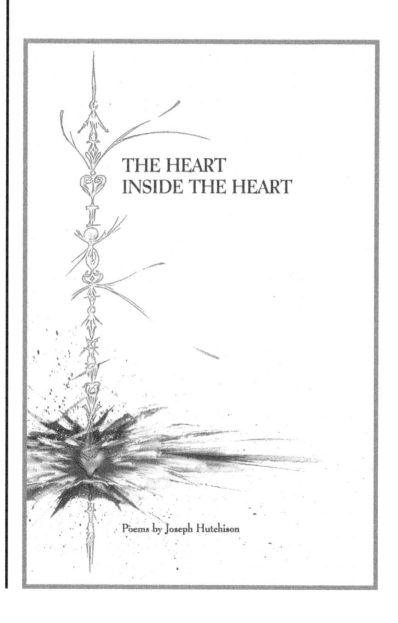

THE HEART
INSIDE THE HEART

Poems by Joseph Hutchison

Naming the Seasons

for David Young

"Autumn"

A sigh of faint surprise. Then
lips lock, shut the tongue
into its shallow tomb.

"Winter"

Tearing wind. Trees flinch
like splinted fingers. Ice
enters us. Night windows hurt.

"Spring"

Dawn spreads wings: downy
rain. Amber welling. Limber
boughs on a blossoming spree.

"Summer"

Bees hum in bloomers. Sun,
then slumber. Someone murmurs.
Only the mirror remembers.

A Story About Fall

for Ted Kooser

Fall arrived in his costume
of frayed husks and ragged fog:
bright, mellow, a bit aloof.
Stayed long past midnight
with his full-moon mask,
cap of glowing clouds
and starry bells. Later,
drunk on wind, he wobbled
through the frigid dark
and passed out, pale
on the frazzled grass;
by dawn, forgetting
how he got there, rose
up and staggered on home.
Now he sits, faintly blue,
thumbing the vivid diary
his lover left behind,
scrapping it leaf by leaf.
Nothing here that lasts,
he muses. *Kind of sad,*
all that foolishness.

Runaway John

John, the willful skeleton,
escaped from his tomb and away did run.
     Clatter-rattle, chatter-rattle,
     click, clack, click—
he ran until his joints felt sick.

He wobbled along as the moon rolled down
like an apple of snow beyond the town.
     Clack-click, rattle-clatter,
     CRASH! John fell
against the wall of a dried-up well

and scattered into the grass. Then day
filled the wood in its whispery way:
     dew-hush, lark-twitter,
     shadowy boughs;
a wind poured over the bony brow,

and out from the skull a low sound came—
a note as hollow as poor John's name.
     Hoot-sound, flute-sound,
     drifting the breeze,
reached only flowers, stones and trees.

Other than these it touched no one,
and never has yet, under sun after sun.
     No matter how fiercely
     you listen at dawn,
you can't hear the moan of Runaway John.

The Metaphysics of Thirst

Beer in a bottle captures
some sun and hides it
in a bubble. To fool thieves conceals
reflections of the fire in others,
in others its image. The true sun
soon gets lost...and the beer
gets worried, gets frantic.

Prying the cap, we hear the brew
sifting, sifting its bubbles. *Heraclitus,*
we muse, and lift the bottle, kiss
its smooth zero...feeling
stars make their chilling escape
into the watery night
of our mouths....

"Leading a Life,"

they say. Each of us a road
and the traveler on it.
Here,

the destination:
each step an arrival,
each step the homecoming.

The Rain
at Midnight

poems by

Joseph Hutchison

Family Planning

A few whiskies into the moping hour
he can almost make himself faint
with the memory: his doctor fishing
for that elusive *vas deferens,* snagging
it—giving it a quick, hard twist. Christ!
He hadn't known those strings fastened
to his eyeballs in back, where the ends
spat like frayed powerlines, making sweat
shower over him like sleet. "Does it hurt?"
crooned the doctor. Snip-snip. "There,
didn't feel a thing, did we." *We?*
He shook his head manfully, spinning
only a moment into the roaring blackness.

But really it had been mostly painless—better
than putting his wife through major surgery,
the gas alone a hazard. Besides, this way
he could drive himself home and lie back
with an ice-pack on his plum-colored scrotum,
letting her pamper his ache like a geisha.
Every three hours she crept to his bed
with tea and a pill, beaming at his proof
that the other woman was gone for good.
(*It* was *proof,* he muses, splashing the Irish
into his glass.) Having nothing to offer
but pleasure, the years ahead seemed clear.
Everything was clearer then. Wasn't it?

Sundown

A globe of fire-glue drooped
from the tube's end: white
hot, then yellow-orange,
then orange as it plumped
with the glassblower's
meticulous breath. It seemed
the turning shaped his airy

gift, the way the world shapes
how we know it. "The sun's
going down" isn't so, but even
astronomers say it; as even those
who can't love find themselves
whispering, "I'll love you
always." *Always*, said the glass

in a crackly voice as it cooled.
Always, it cried years later,
shattered by anger in a year
of loss. *Always*, I find myself
thinking as I write…gazing
out the darkening window,
watching the sun go down.

Punishment

Two lovers with no future
going at it: the bed's headboard
bumps the wall, hung upon which
Van Gogh's manic *Irises* knocks

gently; nails sunk into studs
and plaster grow a little looser.
Such punishment is why the house
will collapse someday, the world

being what it is: a planet
full of lovers with no future—
only *now, now*—and that famous
"it" all of them keep going at.

An Amusing Anecdote

Why did she want to see me now
that our divorce is final? I thought
she would imitate stone, but all
through lunch she's been talkative.
Something about a painting I believe
I've never seen (though she swears
we viewed it together, years ago,
at an Exhibition of Thulean Masters).
Something, too, about the rain—
mention of which sets me trembling, as if
suddenly soaked to the bone. (I can still
hear the shower curtain shrieking
as she rakes it back, remember how
savagely that girl from the office
shrank away behind my shoulder.)
Sucking at my daiquiri, I notice
she's adding milk to her tea—
something she didn't learn from *me*.
(Tea with milk unraveling in it,
like fraying threads of a galaxy, always
reminds me of Northern Europe: Streets
chilled, glistening; a black, polished car
hisses by…"The Third Man Theme"
bleeding from the dashboard radio; fingers
writhing from a sewer grate!) Just then
she laughs, mouth wet. The waiter
has brought our bill—and by mistake
I'm wielding it like a dwarf's bandanna,
mopping the sweat from my eyes.

Three Male Voices

1

Ears flaring red, I'd dive
backward to the floor,
kick and wail. And Mama
would bend to gather me up
sometimes, and sometimes
slap with the flat of her hand,
and sometimes land a fist.
Still, in the end, Mama
always gathered me up,
held me hard against her.

2

What can a man do with the ball
of barbed wire inside his chest?

Call it a heart.
Give it to women.

Let them drop it, the bitches!
Let their mangled hands bleed.

3

I was lifted, sleeping,
like floating on calm water.
Strong, quiet breathing.
We moved through woods.
My legs were so long, dangled
so far down, that my feet
dragged in the black grass.
We moved under leaves,
moonlight splashing
across my closed eyes.
Just before waking
I opened them wide
and gazed a long time
upward at the stony face
of the child who carried me.

The One-Armed Boy

has taught himself to play catch
with the walls of his house.
With great difficulty has learned
to open jars, trap grasshoppers,
write in straight lines. Has,
over time, discovered how
not to hear his mother weeping,
or his father roaring drunk.
Has carefully trained himself
to deflect the cutting
comments of his schoolmates.
If only a saw had gnawed it off!
Or some gigantic shark, as in
his recurring fantasies. If only
he hadn't been born like this.
And yet, near sleep, the arm
that never was reaches out,
touches something even the boy
can't name. Like rain at midnight
falling into a field of poppies, it
gently bathes his non-existent hand.

Strange but True

The asphalt unrolls out of the gray-dirt
flatness daubed with weeds, two lanes queasy
with August heat. Cranked halfway down,
all the windows shudder. The boy's bare feet,
propped on the dash, bathe in the hot gush
from the open wing (this is before conditioned
air, spring-loaded cupholders, stereo FM).
It's late morning, eighty miles from Dubois,
Wyoming.
        Father and son left Denver at dawn
to fish the Wind River, where (they both
know) the boy will barely wet his hook
before the boredom takes over…his casts
turn sloppy, the snags more frequent; his father
will scold, they'll fight; the boy will end up
in the car alone, sullenly thumbing the lurid
paperback he'd bought for a buck in Cheyenne:
Strange But True.
        At this moment, though,
peace. The boy can't sleep, but keeps nodding
off into states of suspension; the wind's boom,
the motor's drone, the road's throaty roar
melt and run together in his skull
until his brain's steeped in warm honey;
so that, when his father speaks, the words
float in from far off like sprays of milkweed—
glimmering, buoyant, faintly surprising
(they've driven in silence for over an hour):
"I wonder," he says, "where the rubber goes
that wears off the tires."
        A mystery
they ponder for a breath or two—then both
grin, start to laugh…until the laughter
floods them with wakefulness, makes
the whole vagueness of Wyoming shift
into focus: flaking highway lines the color

179

of old mustard, greenish bursts of sage,
phone wires and fences loping by, mountains
thick and blue in the distance…and all of it
shining in their watering eyes as they fly—
laughing, father and son—through summer
and the summer of their lives: strange but true.

Something More

He came home smashed.
Seventeen. Shirt and jeans
nubbled with the oddments

of an August evening spent
face-up under a wheeling
willow tree. His buddies

had pressed the full-moon
glow of the doorbell button,
taken off. Then a skewed

square of living room light
opened around him. He
swayed...squinted at her

pinched frown, her blue eyes
scaldingly astonished. "Mom,"
he mumbled, and hauled

the screendoor wide, wobbled
on in. "You'd better get out
of those things," she said.

Next he knew, he'd spilled
his bones into the woozy bed.
But he'd barely started down

the churning spiral into sleep
when a burst of brightness
thumped his shut eyes. She

sank down beside him: "Here."
She turned his ache-stabbed
forehead toward the lamp

and with her thumb tugged at
the corner of his eye. "You can't
sleep with contact lenses in,"

she reminded him. Her palm
warmed his jaw as he gazed
into her altered face; the frown

had yielded to a fiercer look:
half amusement, half pity.
Soon she'd worked out both

shards of plastic, popped them
into her cupped hand. Then
she stood and said, "There.

You sleep. You go to work
in three hours." She switched
off the light, and he watched her

step away, watched her pause
in the doorway as if to say
something more. But as ever,

she let her silence and the dark
comprehension in his heart
speak for them both.

White Owl

A man stares at his life and doesn't know what to do. He feels he must do something…but the car runs fine, the apartment's clean, necessary letters have been written. The leaves in his ex-wife's yard need raking—but that's another life; he needs to do something about *this* one, and he drifts from window to window looking for clues. He snaps the radio on, then off; picks up a pen, and puts it down. A few whiskies later, he nods off in front of the ball game, misses seeing the Cowboys beat the Redskins, though he hears distant battle sounds as he crawls through the forest. He's muddied his face because the moon is full. Thin black boughs lash his cheeks. Somewhere nearby, as a boy, he buried a cigar box full of treasures—and sure enough, a little digging under a willow brings it to the surface: white owl. But the box is empty. Someone's been here ahead of him, like grave robbers at the pharaoh's tomb. The moon sinks beyond a ridge. The noise of battle swells. On the box lid the owl shuffles its snowy feathers, uttering a warm bassoon-like note…the familiar pronoun…utters it with great weariness, as if to say, "So—what more did you expect?"

183

Dusk

Midwinter twilight,
and this urge to open

my coat to the wind.
So I do. I let the cold

worm under my shirt,
creep over my ribcage;

I let it count the bars.
And dusk deepens,

dyes the clouds
of my breath:

no way to stop it—
the darkness I mean.

Bending over My Reflection

The tide pool still, a hand's-depth of crystal,
its black basalt floor gnarled like a brain.
Crabs spider into crevices and out—scant ghosts
waking a swarm of shudders under the water's skin.

One Wave

It seemed one wave
swept forth differently,
with a dark motive. It

hissed about my feet,
kissed at the bones,
the frigid backwash

washing packed sand
out from under them.
At times, it seems

I've never left
that shore. It seems
a wave still gushes

between my ankles,
still wills me
toward the deep;

my toes still clutch,
aching—and I stagger:
I dance for solid ground.

What I Know

Je est un autre.
          —Rimbaud

Tears creep down the upturned face.
My face, although it seems I see it
from across the room. It seems
that I approach the bed and gaze
at the weeping man lying there. I am
sorry about his loneliness and fear,
but I know they will diminish
toward morning when sleep
comes at last. The pillow will be
damp and cold, but sleep will come.

Why, I wonder, can't my knowledge
comfort him? After all, he is me
and suffers only because he refuses
to see me standing in the dark
with what I know.

Black River

You believe you must be beginning again.
The river opens to accept your first step,
and you're into it up to your knees—
the water's wrestle brotherly, bracing.
You start across, shouldering goods
you believe you'll need on the far side.
Waist-deep now. Feeling for rooted stones
through sopping boots. Surely it was here
you crossed before; there is no abyss, no
unknown channels…though the current
does seem swifter than you remember,
and darker (of course, it's only dusk
coming on, staining the air and water;
and the river—you believe—only seems
to be growing wider). Chest-deep now.
Icy water races past your racing heart,
under raised arms that ache to balance
whatever you carry, what you must (you
suddenly understand) be willing to let go.
Chin-deep. Perched on a slippery stone
that shifts with each shivering breath.
No choice but to take the next step—
deeper into the black river, farther
toward the shore of ink-black pines
over which the feverish stars have risen
and the cold comfort of a bone-white moon.

The Ghost

"I know my heart is not enlightened."
—Wang Wei

A mist-haunted grove,
the early dusk arrowed
with light left over

from the late Bronze Age.
Sparks of wetness bend
the deer-waded grass

by the creek that threads
among roots like breath
drawn into a loom

of words. Stillness. Then
the mist lifts; sun-warmth
deepens; and a shadow

stretches from my body,
a ghost of brushed-thin ink.
We stand together now

in silence. Overhead,
spent pine cones sway
like broken temple bells.

The Moonlit Dream

for Jim Bednar

The dream's all voices: hers. "The hundred-faced moon," I would say. Moon out of Lorca, and the rest. But the moon's been walked on in my lifetime and can only be dust now, or nostalgia. Still, all I've learned has come through those voices in the moonlit dream, their swaddling textures. Once a friend put on Jimi Hendrix, saying, "I've taught myself to listen till all I can hear are the scratches. Rock 'n' roll Zen," he grinned, as Hendrix soared into *Foxy Lady*. A fifth of wine later I pressed my cheekbone against the cold linoleum and sank through the basement floor, into the arms of the voices. Far off, some thug was pounding a tin can down over my heart. I wept for my heart among the voices, and their murmuring was a balm to me. "Don't fear the blessing," they sang. "Your soul was meant to be hung in the willows."

Outing on a Gray Day

for George McWhirter

Mais l'instant s'allonge
Qui a profondeur.
　　　　　—Guillevic

Yet if the intervening film
breaks down, it is death.
　　　　　—D. H. Lawrence

I
Through the Marina

This water backed up from
the Fraser River is viscous
as sleep. Upon slippery planks
(lashed to hollow drums) we climb
over sucking, oily ripples
and the creak of fraying knots.
Old nails whimper where we step.
Whatever's sunk here's smeared
by algae—what grim handshake
of withered light?
Only what floats can be
clearly seen: a fish,
bottles, twine, the names of boats
that every gust or raindrop scatters.
Even the kids, hand
in hand with our reflections,
float.
　　　And edging
the narrow inlet, tangled
as genital hair, coils
of barbed wire shiver
with wind, making breath
catch like a ball of down
deep in my chest.

191

Then, from beyond
the skeletal bridge, a cormorant
wheels wildly upward
and, as a steady drizzle starts,
hangs:

black fingers
spread in the rain.

II
Along the Fraser

On the seaward current, the cormorant
cranks back its stiletto head—
then unwinds
three quick strikes. Plucked
out like a pulpy root,
the fish flails
but is sucked down neatly.
And squatting on either side,
the kids touch
my trembling knees.
"Hey,"

I breathe. "Can you sail
stones?" (Nearby, George hefts
a stump and waltzes
it away to the bridge road.) Our first
volleys spook the bird, who alights
down river. Flat as foot soles
more rocks skip across the water,
flip, cartwheel and plunge.
(Returning, George waves blackened
fingers and calls: "Pitch
makes a good fire!")
Grown bored, the kids wander off

behind their father. I too would follow,
if the granite did not fascinate
my bones. Instead,
I kneel here and dip
my hands deep: the jealous
river grabs me by the wrists
like a lover.

III
The Bridge

While George swings firewood
into his car, I wander
on the bridge.

Below, the choked
inlet's iron water.

And floating on a thicket
of rusted wire, another cormorant:
eye of black grease, beak
half-parted like a spent pod,
feathers fingered slick
by rain.
                In its cold
habitat, like a sleeper
swallowed by his bed, I sweat
darkness; vertigo climbs
the thermometer of my throat; spine
willowy as a mangled wing….
I feel I can't turn
back. But calling, George
waves me back.

And I return.

IV
Driving Home

The road under my hunched
body rivers, the ghosted
landscape streaming
over the glass
skin of my reflection.
The fragrance of George's
sap-streaked jacket ripens
the car. *You navigate*
time, its wheels
seem to mutter. *What matters*
is the eye's reach into all
it can't grasp:
water; light; this Earth
you'll enter and enter until
there's no leaving it.
Suddenly, the kids
point from the back seat:
"Look!"

Above the road, a slowly
turning wheel of birds,
the low sky splitting
open as we watch
into canyon on canyon
of radiant white.
And at the flute end
of space:

SUN.
        A numbed
clutch of roots catches
fire in my skull. Like birds
the leaves of my vision
rise up…riding the secret
currents in the air.

On a Used Copy of Witter Bynner's Translation of the *Tao Teh Ching*

for David Lachman

These cigarette ashes smudged
into the gutters of my book
call to mind the one who read,
smoked, contemplated—dog-earing
certain pages, meaning to return.
The copyright notice is 1944:
This is a John Day Wartime Book.
"The sanest man," says this Laotzu,
"takes everything as it comes,
as something to animate,
not to appropriate." Brother,
sister—do you still breathe,
I wonder? Or have you returned
to the root the whole world
flowers from? This book
you lost or mindfully set adrift
discovered me, as it will someday
surely discover others; and since
I breathe, I offer your shadow
this poem as thanks—these words,
these smudges of ash....

Seduction

The mind has a way
of wandering
most when you least
expect it. There it goes,

off the edge, avoiding this
obvious line your eye
dutifully follows—
to what end? To wherever

past each forest a bridge
reaches, then a wall, walls
and roofs. So before you
know it, the mind is

lost in the world, and we
are alone in this dark
room together: nothing
but breathing between us.

The Blue

In memory of Michael Nigg,
April 28, 1969 – September 8, 1995

The dream refused me his face.
There was only Mike, turned away;
damp tendrils of hair curled out
from under the ribbed, rolled
brim of a knit ski cap. *He's hiding*

the wound, I thought, and my heart
shrank. Then Mike began to talk—
to *me*, it seemed, though gazing off
at a distant, sunstruck stand of aspen
that blazed against a ragged wall

of pines. His voice flowed like sweet
smoke, or amber Irish whiskey;
or better: a brook littered with colors
torn out of autumn. The syllables
swept by on the surface of his voice—

so many, so swift, I couldn't catch
their meanings...yet struggled not
to interrupt, not to ask or plead—
as though distress would be exactly
the wrong emotion. Then a wind

gusted into the aspen grove, turned
its yellows to a blizzard of sparks.
When the first breath of it touched us,
Mike fell silent. Then he stood. I felt
the dream letting go, and called,

"Don't!" Mike flung out his arms,
shouted an answer...and each word
shimmered like a hammered bell.
(Too soon the dream would take back

197

all but their resonance.) The wind
surged. Then Mike leaned into it,
slipped away like a wavering flame.
And all at once I noticed the sky:
its sheer, light-scoured immensity;
the lavish tenderness of its blue.

A Midsummer Night's Tennis Match

for Joe Nigg

We're swatting balls
under the floodlights,
over the net (pang
of taut racket strings,
pang in the arm, the heart);
sweat lacquers our backs
in the midnight heat.

The game: to be here
at every stroke, aiming
beyond each other's reach.
The cardinal rule: honor
the lines drawn by others,
their odd ordering of points—
Love, 15, 30, 40—when zero,
one, two, three would do.
And what's this swatting
and sweating for? The night
beyond the light is deep,
and the lines enclose
an emptiness. Yet

the court is a field
where grace appears—not
springing from a score alone,
nor only from strokes perfected,
but from the pangs. Amazing
grace in the rightness
of the pangs.

Brightness and Shadow

Gone

the sweet agitation of the breath of Pan.
—Robert Lowell

She couldn't stay, so he's up with the sun.
He drifts room to room and collects the candles,
vanilla and spice-scented, and cinnamon,
and wildflower, and puts them away.
He snaps shut the oil-bottle's cap (it leaves
a mild fragrance of hyacinth on his fingers)
and twists shut the can of iris-scented talc,
then finds under the sofa the camelhair brush
he used to brush the powder over her breasts,
stomach, hips: all these he puts away. Then
the cassettes they played while making love,
while bantering and laughing, he returns
to their plastic cases, and puts the cases away.
He washes the wine glasses and puts them away.
Then he makes some coffee, toasts some bread,
and sits down to eat...but finds himself
staring out into the courtyard. Rough
wind shakes all the new-leafed branches:
a thrash of green brightness, green shadow.
Yesterday, lying naked near the balcony door,
she followed a blossoming cloud and talked
of childhood; they touched playfully, kissing,
stroking, half-wrestling, tenderly biting....
The memory shakes him like a leafy bough.
Sweet agitation: brightness and shadow.

The Rain at Midnight

Here I am pretending to sleep, but in truth
I'm eavesdropping on the chattering rain,
hearing it gossip in multiple voices
like three beautiful sisters

after dinner, the dessert half-eaten
now that the talk has turned to miseries
of marriage, and bewildering children,
and mothers who knew no better—

and I wonder if they understood
I'm not really asleep, if they felt
my male listening alive in the bright
circle of their concerns…how

they might take it, whether they'd fall
silent, or just go on a bit louder,
a touch more forcefully, knowing I'm there,
knowing who's lurking in their midst—

or maybe they'd simply blend back
into rain, a dark rain, the lull of it,
the sweet nothing noise and the kiss of it,
the tears and the healing sleep of it at last.

from *Sentences*

Sentences

Breath . . .
that clings
briefly
to a sunlit
pane
lives.

Poems by

Joseph Hutchison

"Un Licor Extremo"

This dream

life, gold
as mescal

burning clear
in a bottle;

at bottom:
the cleansing

worm....

Breath...

that clings
briefly
to a sunlit
pane

lives longer
on a cold mirror.

North Country

Love that goes only
part way: the heart

sinking (as they say)
"like a stone" thrown

in some icy lake: each
moment more alone.

In the Labyrinth

My heart's a fist: the dark
thread it tries to follow
keeps slipping away.

Blues

On the swaying black
branches of the sea, whale songs
bloom: blue, then bluer....

Two Starfish
near Siwash Rock

Such cold joy—
the way these two

drowned sailor's
hands

grip land.

Shadows

So the mind wanders:
shadows of blown leaves
toss on the drawn curtain.

Old Faithful

Earth
shuts off:

the fountain
threads
back

into
my head.

Poems from

Thread of the Real

The Earth-Boat

The Satire Lounge

from *Thread of the Real*

Thread of the Real

For George, who shared the path
through the dark wood

Who'd have thought: setting out
from a gap in the seam
between foothills and plains,
a pinch of cocoonish
dust like me

might take wing

northwest and seaward, away
from Nixon's nightbound America
and mine,
        to settle
where vast sounds pour
their profundities into the folds
of B.C.?

Who'd have thought
I'd sleepwalk
into Canada's wooded raininess,

there to be startled awake
by a stogie-puffing

Irish Taoist?

Who was it
who'd led me to believe
there was no magic anymore?

*

He'd tap my head
like a top hat,

213

pull a poem
up from underneath
the false bottom—

    all ears
    and whiskery
    trepidation,
    a feeble motor
    manic in its nest
    of fur—

and pronounce it
crafty as Bugs,
or mystical-whimsical
and soft-hearted
as Harvey.

The dark
and the spotlight
and the music, he'd say,

should amaze both
audience and illusionist,

surprise even jaded
backstage crews
and fellow tricksters

with realities
fresh and unforeseen.

*

The thread of the real
strings our words like beads
together, loops them

around our lover's neck—
they kiss her when she walks.

Or say it's a line of mindfulness
that curves between differently
grained materials, a strand
of cloudy glue squeezed clear
between inlays of rosewood
and blond bay laurel....

Should the thread break,
our words will scatter, turn up
amidst ruins ages hence,
where some bemused digger
may take them for sacred—
and they were.

Hold tight, George said,
to that thread. Follow the ravel
wherever it leads. And if,
in the end, you find that it's real
only for you...well, then:
let that be enough.

*

Everything we cherish—

 Ovid's *Tristia*, Skelton's
 "Night Poem, Vancouver Island,"

 bursts of asters shadowed
 by a horizontal thrust
 of crannied arbutus trunk,

 even your fearsome glimpse
 of cormorant Death,

standing post above the tidal flats,
"drying its shadow on the rocks below"—

is salvage;
as when, reaching

    back through calendars
    unleaving like Goldengrove,

    through moon-haunted mists,

    through lamp-glow folding
    around your writing desk,
    lighting the padded yellow sheets
    of paper your soft-spun voice
    stitched itself across,

    back through complexities
    and perplexities, back
    through silence,
    back through gab,

I touch

a pattern
of unlooked-for
generosity,

long-gone and yet
there still, and always:

deep-hearted pagan spirit
who unbewildered
my tongue,

you taught me to live
on whatever this world
provides—no matter how
high or how low.

And once, as if we'd spent
years together, walking
the Shankill Road of your youth,
you confided, "The old Greek
had it right. The way up
and the way down—
they're the same. Y'see?
Savor the journey."

Snowstorm at Dawn

"It has snowed."

— Francis Ponge, *Memoire d'un sojourn*
à les montagnes de Colorado

Dawn seems an exaggeration: there's a teeming dimness, a gloom or muffled glow alive with swirling palenesses. What light there is creeps up from the strangeness that yesterday was our valley, or down from where the sky must still arch over. Now and then, here and there, the scrappy swarm grows sparse and the southwestward ridge-line appears; gray-green smudges or brushstrokes emerge from the general effervescence...a feeble attempt at distinctness that's quickly overcome by freshly thickening curtains of snowfall....

The flakes themselves soon become weightier. They plummet, wobbling or tumbling, through the rising brightness (we understand the sun has cleared the eastward peaks); and suddenly the storm *reacts*...as when passion—anger or elation, for example—begins to give way to a not-quite-calm...that mildly agitated exhaustion to which we so often resign ourselves, out of which we fashion contentment....

Now the storm-cloth is growing threadbare. A blue brilliance shines through in spots, then in patches. On the opposite mountain, shadows spring from the pines until each tree stands forth in relief, edged with cold fire...as if engraved in gold. Soon enough we notice that the storm has unraveled into shreds of mist, a frosty raggedness adrift in the valley...the way the mind wanders over the floating world when there's nothing more to say.

January Thaw

For a moment or two,
driving through the surprise
mid-winter thaw—all
the streets sheeted
with racing melt-water,

bright ripples like the spaces
between swift lines—

Whitman, Hopkins, Clare—

the car's sun-warm
interior alive
with flickering tree-shadows—
suddenly
there

I was,
floating

above the flood
of words (language,
its abundance: available,
inexhaustible), feeling
my whole being

blossom
in the veins
of the day

as so often in my youth—the old
pulse of onwardness, of sheer
possibility...for just
a heartbeat or two, or three:

world without end
once again.

Kooser Creek

Despite its swiftness, the current's clear.
Grass weaves and unravels under the water.
Fish congregate among cottonwood roots
along the bank, swapping ancient tales
of Heraclitus as a boy—how he liked
to splash all alone in the murky shallows.
Out toward the middle, insect shadows
flicker over sunken plazas of sand.
How refreshing to walk there! But don't
step in unless you mean to get soaked:
the creek floor's further down than it looks.
Besides, big stones have shouldered up
here and there, sturdy enough to cross
over on. Instead, you linger. The interplay
of shade and sun-gleam's mesmerizing,
and you love how the water seems to share
the secrets you need at this very moment,
while saving the rest to tell further on.

Solitaire

In a crooked house, a milk-eyed crone's
turning her ragged cards. No sound

but your breathing: she feels it
as a current in the cards,

a pulse. (Who you are, she
doesn't know, and if she did,

still couldn't tell why her cards
are doors in your life.) The house—

who built it? Who granted this woman
her indifferent power? The cards

turn…and your breath slips
through her fingers like thread

paid out in a labyrinth:
passage on passage,

dark worlds without end.

Winter Sunrise Outside a Café Near Butte, Montana

A crazed sizzle of blazing bees
in the word EAT. Beyond it,

thousands of stars have faded
like deserted flowers in the thin

light washing up in the distance,
flooding the snowy mountains

bluff by bluff. Moments later,
the sign blinks, winks dark,

and a white-aproned cook—
surfacing in the murky sheen

of the window—leans awhile
like a cut lily…staring out

into the famished blankness
he knows he must go home to.

Fox Hollow

The plaque bolted to the brick gatepost
reads: FOX HOLLOW. Two-storey houses,
roofs of shake or salmon-colored tile,
throw-rug lawns, and in each garage
a cloud of gasoline fumes in the shape
of a sport utility vehicle. The streets
curve, shadowless since all the trees
are saplings, trunks taped up like legs
of halfbacks or pre-pubescent gymnasts.

We can hope that on the far side
of the enclave's wall a stubborn fox—
poised amid buffalo grass and burdocks,
amid crushed fast-food boxes—studies
the way lights toward dusk wink on
in the scattered windows. We can hope
he recalls the den of his birth, sharp
musk of his siblings, the dragging
weight of a rabbit in his jaws....

Or let's admit the foxes are gone,
their hollow filled in for a playground.
Let's admit that our enclaves are named
for the absences their existence requires.
Let's ponder these sprinkler systems,
house walls painted in covenant colors,
the steel flags of street signs...each
one—Prairie Dog Lane, Cheyenne Circle—
raised up in memory of a slaughter.

A Dream of Difference

I lift my lamp beside the golden door!
—Emma Lazarus

The ravaged make news only in obits,
but on the front page it's all demagogues,
glassy eyed and misquoting Leviticus,
presidential committees conceived
in denial and dedicated to diversion,
polled majorities deploring condoms,
physicians who make no promises.
America discovers the source of its ills
in whatever is other and seeks to keep it
firmly there. Fags, druggies, Muslims—
let the lamp affix its sickly beam:
the American dream is a dream
of difference that protects the Good;
that is, the deserving ones: you and me.

George W. Bush's First Presidential Press Conference

February 22, 2001

1
When asked about the bombs
lately rained down on Baghdad,
the President pinches his grin
as if toking a half-lit joint: such
hard work, choking back glee.

The aim was to send Saddam
"a clear message," he says,
then pauses, blinking. Crowds
of angels are dancing naked
on the bright pinheads
of his pupils. With a laugh
like a sleeping dog's muffled
bark in a dream, he adds:
"We got his attention."

The dead? The wounded?

Our breathless reporters press
only for bloodless numbers.

How many sorties?
How many tons of explosives?
How many "facilities" taken out?

The hypnotic calculations
of advanced technology....

Logical, of course. Why inquire
after the olive-skinned natives
with their dark-age beards
and burqas, their names
that twist our tongues? Names
make rolling their deaths

225

into the running total
a painful exercise. And pain
impedes the pursuit of happiness.

The cameras flash and whirr;
our eyelids mimic the TV's flicker;
we succumb, nod off….

2
Asphalt lullabies beneath us
in the American dream. The car purrs
and glides; the radio anoints us
with hymns to young love, and we
sing along in our cracked falsetto.
In the American dream, music
is all road music, the road ahead
always clear. But soon
another voice rises, ghosting in
from another channel, or somewhere
off the dial. At first it's faint. *Why
are they dying?* Then stronger,
more insistent. *Because
we have so few tears falling
on our own hands.* The truth of it
showers us with cold panic. How far
are we going exactly? Who the hell
is it, driving the car—

3
The churning
engine in our chest
startles us awake,
fingers gripping
the chair arms. Bush's
performance still burns
coolly on the tube.

Just hold on, we think. Soon
we'll be rescued by the bland
chatter of commentators,
the balm of beer ads. But now
is now: there's no escaping
the carefully mangled language
of power, the President's
unearned bravado, the press
descanting like a choir
of castratos.

Now,
looking down at our hands'
whitened knuckles,
we see that tears must bathe them
in a not-too-distant future
when our wheels go keening
down the new-laid road,
and all the maps are tattered,
and the highway signs are flying
invisibly by as we make
yet one more sentimental journey,
hurtling blindly through "the fog of war."

Tests of Faith

1

I slaughtered my first infidel,
but only after showing him
what mercy the Lord demands.
Go on, I whispered. *Say goodbye
to that wife of yours.* The man

sobbed into the hooded eye
of the camera, stammering love.
Later: two hours of fervent prayer,
five of celebration. My brothers'
cheers broke like spring rain

over my buzzing head, bathed
my fevered face. I'd begged
to be given a vision of heaven,
and had my answer: the gash
parting thick lips beneath

the gliding blade, the shudder,
the seizure of breathlessness,
the sanctified release. My hand
made rock by the strength of God.
This righteous hand!

2

I strapped my first jihadi down,
strapped down jaw and brow
to make him gape, gagged him—
then let the cold water pour. *Go on!*
I roared. *Tell us again how great*

Allah is! Hanson circled, aimed
the Handycam; the hajji thrashed,
gasped, retched—how many times?

I lost count. But, at last, he lapsed
against the board, mother-naked,

a void. *Fuck,* I said. But Hanson
had a plan. We laid the guy on ice
in a ration crate, pending the next
trash run. Later: two hours toasting
American ingenuity at the Baghdad

Country Club, 'til Hanson's head
lolled to the table. I drank on,
thanking Christ the Army drummed
every weakness out of my heart.
This well-trained heart!

3

I strangled my first poet
in the mirror. The nightmare's
pulsing alarm conjured up
a thudding 'copter, the broad
blade of its searchlight cleaving

my tongue's hoof. *The most
horrible things,* says Linh Dinh,
*become mere spectacles to the true
outsider.* Which side of my skin
is best to write on? Will I turn

into a tattoo addict, or a habitué
of opium dens? *Read an American
account of the war, and you see
how excited the writer is. He is
almost gleeful.* Linh, don't tell me

brutality's the *lingua franca* now!
I feel sick gutting a fish. Caught

in the gunship's shadow, I grieve
hearing news about the divorce
of Signifier and Signified.

4

I signed the executive order,
and the mosque was crushed.
I (another I) whispered a code,
and weeks later yet another I
climbed a shattered ladder

made of bomb-vest fragments
toward a hive full of virgins.
I voted billions for the Pentagon
in exchange for certain photos.
In lieu of the news, I recited

a teleprompter's lies. I marched
for peace, but no one could read
my sign's scribbled Aramaic.
My brothers and I surrounded
our whorish sister and broke her

with stones. My taxes rained
down like fire on the orphans.
Sometimes I wake in the night
and think, *The war is over.*
But another I remembers.

Field Notes Concerning the Bomb

The bald, jug-eared foreign policy expert advocates bombing Tehran.
The ex-Director of Mossad wants to bomb Beirut or Damascus, or both.
The CEO of Raytheon aims to grow the lucrative cluster bomb market.

*

The audience enjoys hooting and jeering when the stand-up comic bombs.
The gamer whoops when the dusky bomber explodes in a cloud of red pixels.
When Wile E. Coyote gets bombed to ash, the toddler cries, "Beep beep!"

*

The Sudanese med student wants to bomb the arrogant Danish cartoonist.
The talk radio fanatic suspects his neighbor's gardener of planting a bomb.
The born-again President dreams of cramming a bomb up the Devil's ass.

*

The émigré poet begs Jesus to bomb the dictator who raped her voice.
The pilot bombs a mud-brick hovel, then flies off above the ascending dust.
Glimpsing himself in a lobby mirror, the Jakarta Hilton bomber hesitates.

*

Its builders, dealers, devotees and victims mean nothing to the bomb.
The bomb needs nothing and desires nothing—not even to explode.
Anti-Buddhas: each bomb's awakening makes even emptiness suffer.

Dark Matter

for Tom Auer, in memoriam

On my way to your wake, stuck at a stoplight,
out of the ether this talk radio voice drifts—
some cosmologist, keen on deep space:

> *The Hubble telescope's found light*
> *in just four percent of the universe.*
> *The rest is full of something we call*
> *"dark matter."*

Odd, how the notion relaxes my knotted throat.
Everything must go! Cities. Farms. Nations.
Earth itself will be slag—a frozen tear....

The light blinks green and I stamp the gas.
Across town your friends are gathering now,
bringing stories about your love of books
and your daily kindness. Among the heartfelt
bromides, the helpless shrugs and far-off stares,
I'll know your erasure's just a red-shift blur,
your life—like all lives—a stray particle
sparked off by the night machine....

For a mile or more it seems almost all right,
until the station veers from talk to music—
piano waves and a salt-scarred voice:

> *I'm leavin' my fam'ly,*
> *leavin' all my friends.*
> *My body's at home*
> *but my heart's in the wind...*

Rolling blues that would make you sway.
Would have made, I mean. Just months ago.
Back when it seemed we had nothing but light.

The Mist of Sustenance

Lost Time

At the end of our last visit, I waved
as the car slowed away from the curb,

and Dad waved back—straightened
in his wheelchair where he'd parked it
at the living room's picture window,

and raised both arms and moved them
like a signalman wielding invisible flags
on a ship's sinking deck. With a shock

I saw that he was waving to a vanishing
image of himself, signaling in distress,

at sea in a mirror made of lost time.

*

Days

The backs of my father's hands,
splashed with bruises…the dream
had scrubbed them clean. His heart
was healed, and the raw gravel
grinding down his knee joints
had been washed away. I thought
that for the first time in years
his ears could catch sparrow song,
chitter of squirrels, faint breath
of a breeze in the shadowy trees
around his garden. I saw him crouch
to test a tomato's redness, then stand
up easily, giving it a few days more.
Months later that simple image

can sting my eyes until they glisten,
seeing how the dream had granted him
days without end.

*

Riddles for My Father

> *Whatever we see when awake is death;*
> *when asleep, dreams.*
> —Heraclitus

He began in Colorado.
Anyplace he loved was home.
His breath scarred by cigarettes
was a rough-barked branch;
an orphaned owl hunched there,
amber eyes cradling a banked fire.

The moon was new all of his life.
The stars trafficked in secrets.

Only the earth woke in his hands
that were strong as barn-door hinges,
and he savored the give and take
of seed and harvest. His nightmare:
an upright pitchfork forgotten
deep in a mound of hay.

But always there was a horse
snorting in its damp stall,
and a saddle on the stall rail,
and not far off some mountains,
and canyons a man might live
another life in, and rivers he might
step into and out of at will....

(He'd never have heard Heraclitus
in those lines, for who in our family
would have loved such riddles
but me? I knew he'd declare them
dark and not to be trusted—so
I always held my tongue.)

Now he sleeps in the earth,
in that long dreamless house
clods drummed down on
like hooves. His face
is a new moon, and all
that was starry in him flies
like a dry beam of light
away from me. His hands
lay like broken sheaves
at his sides.

I'm awake.
And Heraclitus
is ashes in my mouth.

*

Cloudy Night Window

The mound of lentils, freshly washed, dripped in a gray aluminum
colander in the sink while his father did magic with the stock-pot:
bouillon cubes, barley, carrots, half-moons of celery, fat tomato
chunks, the translucent petals of yellow onion, the rich mystery of
spices. Above the sink, elm branches crazed the west-facing window,
sifted the bleak last light as it drained away beyond the broken wall
of peaks. February? Early March? Still winter for sure. (It's winter
where his father's grave steeps in the rain of other mountains, in
a future that is now and yet seemed so remote then—impossible,
in fact.) He lifted the colander and shook the lentils into the pot,

235

quelling its boil, then stirred and stirred with a long wooden spoon until the broth was roiling again. He turned the burner knob to low and laid the lid in place. Soon enough they'd all sit down at the blue Formica table, the bowls and spoons already set out, and breathe in the earthy steam. The night window would be cloudy then, thick with the mist of sustenance that hid the darkness from them.

*

A Celebration

The revolving door gasped
behind me, and I drifted onward
into the room: the carpet plush,
a ceiling lost in vaulted shadows.
On the far wall, a milky glow
poured through high windows.
The celebration was in my honor,
but I wished I wasn't there—all
the faces vague, the hubbub
churning. In an open sitting area
(sofa, chairs, the table-lamps dim)
Mom stood, clutching her purse,
eyes alive with coy mischief,
her smile haunting as a fox's.
Before I could speak, she glanced
off to her right, and I saw him—
taller than me for the first time
in thirty years. His changed skin
shone like moon-washed snow,
his hair grown thicker and white
as apple blossoms. I thought
to ask him how he'd come there,
but suddenly he was cloaked
in a cloudy light. In silence
I stepped toward him, a calm

236

overtaking me like those summer
dawns we'd crawl from our tent
to fish Jakey's Creek, a barren mile
from where it eased into the cold
Wind River. The closer I came,
the more Dad loomed. Reaching
up, I slipped my arms around
his waist and touched my cheek
to his stomach's warmth. He said
nothing, but cupped his hands
lightly over my shuddering
shoulder blades, as if gentling
a horse—and I clung to him.
Against my will I clung to him,
as he could no longer cling to me.

Comfort Food

Long Distance

His mother knows
who but not where
he is. She warns
into the phone, "Don't
rake leaves too long,
you'll hurt your back."
Out his window,
leafless piney ridges,
the farther ranges
snowbound. "Don't
worry now," he says.
"I'll be careful."

Next time she knows
where but not who.
"You never *listened*,"
in a child's voice.
"It's me," he begins.
She snaps: "You think
I don't *know* that?"
And suddenly she's
chatting about the rain
and fog out her window,
there at the far other
end of the line.

*

Breath

The world enters
us as breath. We

return it to itself
as breath. When

we're done with
the world, where

(he wonders) does
all that breath go?

*

A Travelin' Woman

The last words his mother said to him
were (as usual) long distance. Freed
at last from the doctors' clutches,

delivered by wheelchair into the human
tenderness of hospice, she exulted
into the phone: "I'm a travelin' woman!"

"Where you headed?" he said, buoyed
by her joy. "Where?" she laughed.
"I don't know. Timbuktu!"

*

*Dream Image After
the First Good Cry*

westwarding river—
red-gold shreds of Sun scattered
on it and in it

*

Open Casket

She's a stranger, though he has to agree

they've done a beautiful job with her hair,
and yes she looks peaceful, out of pain,

and the silk blouse under the black sweater
shines like the petals of a sun-struck lily,
and the hands, one atop the other, look

as if he'd held them. Knowing he doesn't
know this stranger, though, he turns away,

eyes shut tight to remember his mother.

*

Going On

They knew her breath would stop,
as her husband's breath had stopped.
As people by the thousands every day
stop, breathing the world back one

last time into itself. Like all mourners,
they felt the world itself should stop.
But no. The world simply took her
last breath back—then began to share

it among them in the form of weeping.
Like a sacred bread. This sorrow bread.
Can this be the secret, then? The breath
they all had shared with her so long

still here, in the world—the world's
going-on keeping it in circulation?
Small wonder they savor the ache of it:
the unstopped breath of a mother's love.

*

Rereading "Hear"

> *after Lorine Niedecker*

Twenty-some years
back he sounded out
her transcription of
mourning doves
     You
ah you
   her mother
gone gravely still

Only now has he
come to hear those
doves her way:
     True
too true
   he longs
to say—

To whom?

*

Comfort Food

A fifty-something crying in the dairy aisle,
lost in a dream of his dead mother. Grief

241

welled up in him, "out of nowhere"
(as they say), and now he's a spectacle.

At least his display turns out to be brief.

He smiles abjectly a moment, "gathers
his wits," lets loose a broken sigh—
then picks out the goods he came to buy.
Butter. Cheese. The whole milk of childhood.

From a Swaying Hammock

With a raw squawk the raven breaks
his glide and alights on a pine's

spring-like branch. What peaks gleam
in his onyx eye? What fat anoints his beak?

When I doze, it seems I hear my name
picked apart by his artful caws,

feel the combs of his claws
prowling among my graying hairs.

How can I sleep with him perched there?

Mortality

Hard to imagine yourself
in the ground…a shabby mess
of broken spindles, the loom
that cranked out the cloth of you
smashed, scattered—and somewhere
the ego sputtering its rage.

You can hear it now—railing
like a mill-town dowager
piqued, let's say, by the country's
fraying moral fiber. Her spotted fist
gavels the tea-table, making
the bone teacups clatter.

"Oh! The very idea!"

Ritual

Meloxicam to soothe the angry disk between L2 and L3, pinched and bulging like a bitten tongue. Prilosec to save the stomach from the ravages of Meloxicam and to keep down the Resveratrol (an oblong lump of compressed soot said to keep the blood vessels pliant and cancer at bay). Also a capsule of fish oil the warm color of tequila *añejo*, and vitamin C of course, and a packeted pile called Nature's Code, whose purpose I can't recall. Nevertheless, I wash the whole handful down every morning with a half-sweet, half-biting antioxidant berry-juice mixture made to scape chemical rust off the walls of my many millions of aging cells. As in the past, in eras rife with superstition—irrational, unscientific, fearful of demons, djinns, ghosts of ancestors, rival gods: this irritable reaching after time and health, this hapless genuflection to the Invisible.

Yoga

for Melody

The teacher guides their breath
into a depth his doesn't like
at first. He lets her make
his lungs plump up, then

lead his body into Downward
Facing Dog. The class has seen
what her body does; but his—his
just isn't made the same. Her glance

argues, *All you lack is discipline.*
Why? Those years in school,
outwitting bullies, making grades,
escaping into books—didn't his body

bear him like a mule on its back?
Suddenly, tremors invade his arms—
but the teacher's fierce. "Hold it. Hold it."
He breathes into his shaky limbs

because she says he can…breathes
(it hits him) because *she* breathes
so beautifully. It must be *her*
he wants to breathe in! "Good,"

she announces. "Child's Pose."
He collapses with the rest, folded
around his secret. Or do the others
sense how intently he listens

as her naked feet brush the bare
wood floor? Now she halts, inches
from his tucked head. "Just relax,"
she says. And he tries. He tries!

"And don't forget to breathe."

Unfinished Stories

for Shannon

Nine may be too old for this,
my wife's look suggests.
My eyebrows crumple.
Really? Nine's too old?

Let's see.

We snuggle her between us
like when she was seven,
plump the pillows behind us,
pull the covers up under our chins.

"A peanut-butter-and-jelly sandwich
was walking through the forest…"

We take turns inventing
its sandwichy adventures.
It can eat and be eaten,
be squashed by an elephant,
marry a telephone or a dill pickle,
play the trombone at a monkey party.

(Mention of monkeys
gives us permission to jut
our jaws and puff out
our cheeks,
scratching and grunting,
screeching like crazed violins.)

Sometimes we wander off
with a skunk or a tightrope walker
and forget where we left the sandwich.
Poor sandwich! Its peanut butter
melting in the broiling sun
by an empty highway in Arizona,
strawberry jelly leaking from the crust
where it scraped against a cactus….

247

We pass the story around
a good long while sometimes.
Sometimes just a turn or two
brings us to the end.

"*The* end!" she announces,
and we send the sandwich off
on another adventure. Or she says,
"I'm tired," and my wife says,
"Go get in your bed."

Tonight it's tiredness.
We leave the sandwich
under a striped umbrella
on a Mexican beach.

I get a kiss, as always,
but Gramma tucks her in
and rubs her back. Soon
her breathing relaxes;
her face grows soft as a rose.

My wife crawls back in bed,
and we lay awake awhile.

The story still glows in our heads,
but it casts a few shadows, too.
Some not too distant day
she'll say, "Oh Gramma, Grampa—
let's not tell that silly story!"

After that our sandwich
will have no more adventures.
It will vanish in the underworld
of unfinished stories....

A world
very much like this one.

Sacred Stories

Breezy golden light
on the mountain.
Breath by breath,

you climb the rope
of listening and vision
down into the valley,

where the pine-tree
people have already
slipped into a tall,

swaying sleep, while
(in their slim shadows)
the grass people lean,

whispering their most
sacred story: how bleak
this valley was before

their ancestors sailed
an ocean of wind
into its barren folds.

*

Your ancestors came
from Germany via Ukraine,
from Ireland and Scotland.
Dirt farmers, mostly,

mostly half-assed about it,
buying rocky ground (sight
unseen, but cheap), then
trundling west in Conestogas,

iron-jawed women birthing
and burying along the trail.
Wherever they settled, they'd
one day head to town and glare

249

into a lens for a family portrait.
What can you buy with joy,
their lampblack eyes would ask,
on this enemy Earth?

*

Here where Arapaho and Ute
hunted deer in summer, cut poles
for tents, told sacred stories—here
your people platted cramped parcels,
hammered cabins out of scabrous

pine logs, so that moneyed types
could flee the flatland swelter
and odious foreign laborers. Then:
1929. At big desks of burnished oak,
ruined men pressed pistol barrels

to their heads, leaving only a stench
of saltpeter and scorched pomade.
Soon the elite sanctuary's gates
were flung wide to almost anyone
with cash. If not for those shattered

Easy Street fortunes, there'd be no
you pondering these pines, that grass,
that ginger-furred fox, that Taoist
flash of a magpie into the leafy brush.
Why this melancholy, then? You grasp

the meaning of your past, the present
with its evening sun bleeding down
beyond the ridge. No stories here
mention you. But true to your class,
you keep on dreaming of being *let in.*

from *The Earth-Boat*

THE EARTH-BOAT

Joseph Hutchison

Mayan Riviera: Advice for Travelers

The sea wind seldom weakens here,
but when it does, the *chaquistas* come.

No-see-ums. Bite-marks suddenly pimple
your skin, but don't you scratch that itch.

Scratching only makes the little bumps
weep out a sticky, blood-tinted tear.

Restrain yourself. Slather on the aloe.
Lie in a beach chair, covered head to toe.

A fresh wind will come, and a fresh dawn
rubbing its balm on the crawling waters.

Guanábana

After hurricane Gilbert, this place
was only shredded jungle. Now
it's Jesús and Lídia's *casa*,

built by him, by hand, weekends
and vacations, the way my father
built our first house. Years

we've watched the house expand,
two rooms to three, to four, to five.
The yard, just a patch of gouged

sand and shattered palmettos once,
is covered now in trimmed grass,
bordered by blushing frangipani

and pepper plants—jalapeños,
habaneros—and this slender tree
Jesús planted three years back,

a stick with tentative leaves then
out of a Yuban coffee can, but now
thirty feet high, its branches laden

with *guanábana*—dark green
pear-shaped fruit with spiky skin
and snowy flesh, with seeds

like obsidian tears. Jesús
carves out a bite and offers it
on the flat of his big knife's blade:

the texture's melonish, the taste
wild and sweet—like the lives
we build after hurricanes.

The Earth-Boat

The ocean's susurrus....
Now and again a resonant boom.
In its sun-soaked pod the brain
ripens. The Earth-Boat:
for a few breaths
we can feel it drifting.

Black-Footed Albatross

Just where the sliding tide shreds
into whitish tatters on the shore,
an albatross stands—draggled
wings cranked wide, the feathers
like charcoaled streaks fanned out
in the late day wind, each foot
a splash of ink on the sand.

We creep close, near enough
to touch—and snap his picture.
A boy prances and flaps his arms,
but the bird doesn't scare. He stares
out to sea, shadow stretched thin
on the wave-pummeled beach, beak
uplifted like a brujo's stick finger.

He must be dying, someone says.
But this creature's never heard
of Coleridge. When the time
feels right, he thrusts himself
two quick steps forward and up,
lifting and veering over the swells
close in, then the far whitecaps.

The next day he's back, jet-eyed,
imperturbable. Is this a private
ritual? Or a kind of annunciation?
I can almost hear him: *There are many*
worlds in this world, each alive
with many gods. Mine go by names
your tongue is too thick to pronounce.

Photograph from a Caribbean Beach

for Melody

She peeks out through palm leaves,
leaning from behind the whitewashed,
shade-streaked trunk. Your first glance
might miss her—her crimson blouse
could pass for a splash of bougainvillea.
But suddenly there she is.
                                    Some images
seem to brim over their moments in time.
Take this palm tree's lacework shadow,
rippling across the wind-ruffled,
raw-sugar sand, the way her breath
can sometimes brush the tender skin
along my neck. The longer I look,
the more familiar that sun-washed wall
in the background feels: I've touched
a wall just like it inside her, slipping
through sometimes like a radio wave,
other times being gently admitted
like moonlight, or a scented breeze
strayed in from the sea.
                                    Luck's any gift
we don't deserve. Her eyes, for example.
You can't really tell (hidden as it is
behind sunglass lenses), but that shy,
inviting gaze is meant for me.

Voice of the Fountain

for John Ransom and Barbara Mastej

1

Evening into night we sipped
peppery wine in the garden,

caverned in vines and leaves
edged with mood-light colors.
Our voices and the mazy

voice of the fountain
mingled, wandering out

over the moon-mottled grass.
Now held its breath, held
past and future in abeyance,

turned them to pure fragrance:
green ginger, ocean, stars....

2

Toward midnight we stood
for goodbyes...but lingered,

gabbing, till John bent down
by the ivied fence like some
lanky old-time god, and flicked

off first the tinted lights, then
the fountain. A shock, hearing

the water silenced that we'd all
silently agreed to believe (that,
looking back, I still believe)

had come bubbling up fresh,
fresh from the heart of the Earth.

from *The Satire Lounge*

To Poets Who Whine About
the Inadequacy of Language

If you distrust words
so much, why not
shut up? Why waste
the sacrificed flesh
of trees, or strew your
anemic traces across
our computer screens
(each pixel lit by burning
400-million-year-old
ferns and trilobites,
or butchering big rivers
with the blades of turbines)?
You'd deplete the Earth
to trumpet your faithlessness?
Why not simply learn
to paint, or play the flute,
or bow in bewitched
silence over a whirling
potter's wheel?
Words don't serve
because you won't serve
them. So: *Get thee hence!*
And don't let the sacred
door of the dictionary
hit you in the ass.

Uncles

A Thanksgiving poem

Uncle Walt drank German beer,
  Uncle Wystan whiskey.
Uncle Dylan drank whatever
  made his tongue feel frisky.

Uncle Pablo savored eels;
  Uncle Osip, stones.
Uncle Seamus—cabbage and sloes
  boiled with marrow bones.

Uncle Willie dreamed in a tower,
  Uncle Rob in a shack.
Uncle Wally dreamed at the office
  of peignoirs and birds that were black.

Uncle Bill loved many women,
  Uncle Frank loved men.
Uncle Jack loved anyone
  who'd stimulate his pen.

These and other uncles come
  to visit once a year.
We munch a roasted bird with them;
  they toast themselves and cheer.

In the living room we men doze off,
  beguiled by the loud TV.
The aunts who cooked the meal for us,
who drank and ate and dreamed with us,
  study us silently.

The Poet Tenders His Apologia in Terms He Hopes His Son Will Understand

for Brian

My love for poetry,
I tell him, goes back
to a kids' cartoon.
Rocky and Bullwinkle.

Right, he says.

Really! Rocky
the Flying Squirrel
and his sidekick,
Bullwinkle J. Moose,
find themselves lost
in a desert. The sun's
broiling, sky white.
They're crawling.
Their red tongues
drag the sand. Then
this tall dune rises
in front of them,
and a thought bubble
pops up, tied to both
their heads: a palm tree
bends inside it, over
cool blue water.
It's too much! They
scramble to the top,
but on the other side—
no oasis. Not even
a twist of cactus.

Empty desert,
he says. I get it.

But he doesn't,
so I tell him: Now

the narrator speaks up.
William Conrad!
You know—classic
voiceover artist?
Radio's Matt Dillon.

Matt Dillon, I almost
hear him thinking.
Something About Mary.

Gunsmoke, I explain.
Before James Arness.

He sighs, my son.

Well—imagine it,
I say. Conrad's voice
booming like God's.
*Our heroes looked out
over miles and miles
of miles and miles.*

I let the words drift
off into the sheer
openness of childhood.

Not *his* childhood,
though. He gives me
a quick, pinched look,
shakes his head.

Poetry, I shrug.
He rolls his eyes, and I'm
moved to repeat (with
more emotion
than either of us likes):
Poetry!

264

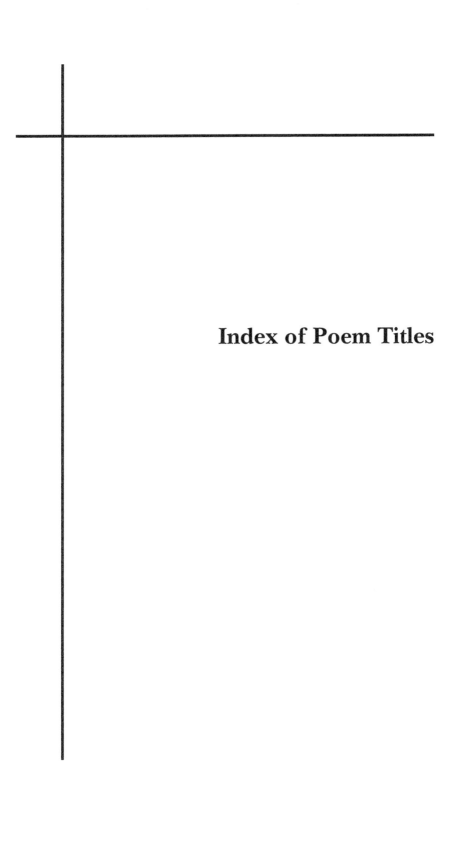

Index of Poem Titles

Acknowledgments

The author gratefully acknowledges the publications in which some of these poems, often in different versions, first appeared.

Able Muse: "Touch"
The Agni Review: "The Gift"
The Chariton Review: "William Matthews"
Colorado Central Magazine: "Revenant"
Concerning Poetry: "Meditation"
Concise Delight: A Magazine of Short Poetry: "May's first mosquito," "purple-haired shop girl," "rain-steps at midnight"
Cutthroat: "Meltdown"
Elevated Living: "The Other Life" (under the title "Here and Now")
The Fiddlehead: "Sense and Absence"
FutureCycle Poetry: "The Things That Carried Them"
Gulfstream: "Talking in Sleep"
Images: "Milkweed on a Windy Spring Day"
Io: "Greeley, Colorado: Sunday Evening Scene"
JuxtaProse Literary Magazine: "The Bat Man" and "Watch Repair"
Kentucky Review: "A Conflict Photo"
The Lampeter Review: "Ode to Something"
Mad Blood: "Crayoned Rainbow" (in an earlier version)
The New Salt Creek Reader: "Intrograph"
Northeast: "snow comes on in gusts," "cliffside daisies swing," "iron graveyard gate," "Suburban Housewife Eating a Plum," and "The Boutonniere"
The Perpetual Bird: "A Bust of Janus Speaks"
Pilgrimage: "Dream Bird"
Poet & Critic: "Fly, He Said" and "Inside My Life"
Poetry Salzburg Review: "The Lifting Bird"
Poets for Living Waters: "The Gulf"
Prism International: "The Ancestral Shore"
Santa Fe Literary Review: "Sea Dream"
SOL: English Writing in Mexico: "Glimpse"
The Sou'wester: "The Greyhound Station: Midnight"
unFold: Earlier versions of "nightfall bus," "windowed snow," and "high-country storm wind"
Verse-Virtual: "At Willamette National Cemetery" and "Crayoned Rainbow" (revised)

"Leaving the Financial District" and "The Greatest Show on Earth" appeared in the anthology *American Society: What Poets See* (Future-Cycle Press, 2012).

"Auger," "First Bird at First Light," and "The Gulf" appeared in the anthology *Weatherings* (FutureCycle Press, 2015)

"heron on stick legs" and "cliffside veined with ice" appeared in the anthology *Lifting the Sky: Southwestern Haiku and Haiga* (Dos Gatos Press, 2013).

"Watch Repair" was presented as part of the Buntport Theater Company's performance, "Son of Very Short Stories" on March 7 and 13, 2015, held respectively at Colorado's Su Teatro Cultural and Performing Arts Center in Denver and at Chautauqua Community House in Boulder.

"The Map" appeared in the anthology *A Ritual to Read Together: Poems in Conversation with William Stafford* (Woodley Press, 2014).

"Milkweed on a Windy Spring Day" appeared in the anthology *Sight Unseen* (Steve Grout, ed., 1978).

"Greeley, Colorado: Sunday Evening Scene" appeared in *Io Anthology: Literature, Interviews, and Art from the Seminal Interdisciplinary Journal, 1965 -1993* (2015).

"Revenant" appears in *The Phoenix: An Unnatural Biography of a Mythical Beast*, by Joseph Nigg (University of Chicago Press).

Thanks as well to the artists whose cover art for individual collections graphically captured the spirit of each volume pictured in the pages of this book:

Patricia Miller, www.patriciamillerfineart.com (*The Undersides of Leaves* and *House of Mirrors*)

John Ransom, www.johnransomla.com (*Bed of Coals, The Heart Inside the Heart, Sentences,* and *The Earth-Boat*)

Thanks to friends, teachers, and editors whose advice and support over the years helped to shape the poems in this book: Melody Madonna, George McWhirter, Vernice Van Duzer, James Roome, Frances Roome, Jim Bednar, Gary Schroeder, Joe Nigg, Esther Muzillo Nigg, David Lachman, Ted Kooser, John Judson, Tom Auer, Marilyn Auer, Ray Gonzalez, Reg Saner, Skip Baldwin, Ed McManis, Rita Kiefer, Sandra S. McRae, Jim Keller, Murray Moulding, Kathi Bernier, William Zaranka, Jared Smith, Bill Tremblay, Janice Hays, Pamela Haines, Nancy Andrews, Thomas R. Smith, Judith Rafaela, Nancy Fay, Caleb Seeling, Diane Kistner, Robert S. King, Jessica Sudborough Graustein, Rose Auslander, Alex Blackburn, Victoria McCabe, Steve Grout, Gary Pacernik, Ron Slate, James Moore, Patricia Hampl, David Spicer, Joseph Bruchac, Ralph Gustafson, Robert Gibbs, John Gill, Richard Grossinger, Lindy Hough, Joseph Parisi, Lisa Steinman, David Giannini, Firestone Feinberg, Scott Wiggerman, Constance Campbell, Becca J.R. Lachman, Lowell Jaeger, Sudasi Clement, Michelle Meyering, and everyone else whose names have eluded my tattered mental dragnet.

About the Author

photo by Kimberly Anderson

Joseph Hutchison, Poet Laureate of Colorado 2014-2018, was born in Denver, Colorado, and grew up in the northwestern-most neighborhood of the city. He was a founding editor of the literary magazine *Pendragon* and co-founder of Wayland Press, a literary publisher that for more than a decade produced books of both poetry and fiction. He is the author of 16 collections of poems, including *The Satire Lounge, Marked Men, Thread of the Real, Bed of Coals* (winner of the Colorado Poetry Award), and the Colorado Governor's Award volume *Shadow-Light*. He also co-edited, with Andrea Watson, the FutureCycle Press Good Works anthology *Malala: Poems for Malala Yousafzai* (all profits to the Malala Foundation), and with Gary Schroeder the anthology *A Song for Occupations: Poems About the American Way of Work*.

For more than 20 years he made his living as a commercial writer but recently became Director of the Arts and Culture program at University College, the University of Denver's adult and continuing education college, where he has taught as an adjunct for many years. Despite his current academic position, he considers himself a community poet and strives to write for readers who may or may not have graduate degrees, using language that is at once direct and layered. His poems are guided by expressive necessity rather than whatever literary theory happens to be ascendant at the moment.

Joseph has two children, Susannah and Brian, and lives with his wife, Iyengar Yoga instructor Melody Madonna, in the mountains south-west of Denver.

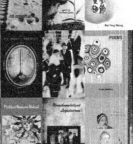

CPSIA information can be obtained at www.ICGtesting.com
Printed in the USA
BVOW08s0050080716

454831BV00002B/4/P